Carefree Cooking

EASY RECIPES FOR BUSY PEOPLE

Carefree Cooking

EASY RECIPES FOR BUSY PEOPLE

Weight Watchers

ANN PAGE-WOOD

NEW ENGLISH LIBRARY

For information about the Weight Watchers classes,
contact: Weight Watchers UK Ltd, Kidwells Park
House, Kidwells Park Drive, Maidenhead, Berks SL6
8YT. Telephone: (0628) 777077

Art Director: Roger Judd
Photography: Simon Smith
assisted by Thierry Guinovart
Home Economist: Ann Page-Wood
Styling: Kathy Man

British Library Cataloguing in Publication Data is
available

First published in Great Britain 1990

Published by New English Library,
a hardcover imprint of Hodder and Stoughton,
a division of Hodder and Stoughton Ltd,
Mill Road, Dunton Green, Sevenoaks,
Kent TN13 2YA
Editorial Office: 47 Bedford Square,
London WC1B 3DP

Photoset by Rowland Phototypesetting Ltd,
Bury St Edmunds, Suffolk

Printed in Great Britain by BPCC Hazell Books,
Aylesbury, Bucks

CONTENTS

INTRODUCTION

There can be very few people who haven't at one time or another said, 'I'm going on a diet', but how many people stick to their enthusiastic intentions of giving up sweets, lashings of cream or nibbles of cheese? Usually the first few days go well but then boredom and frustration set in and the old habits return. Weight Watchers have devised an eating plan which not only aims to help with weight loss and control, but also provides information, group support and delicious recipes which have been devised and tested for their members. The importance of a well-balanced and varied diet is recognised, and so restricted quantities of many foods and drinks, such as chocolate and alcohol, are included in meals throughout the book.

High-quality produce should also be used and the points to note should be followed when selecting and preparing food.

The Selections given at the end of each recipe apply only to members of Weight Watchers following the Weight Watchers Food Plan.

POINTS TO NOTE

MEAT

Buy the leanest meat possible. Always trim all visible fat from meat before cooking and, if the recipe is suitable, remove the skin. Obviously it is sometimes more sensible and convenient to do this after cooking, for example when roasting a joint. Always place meat or poultry on a rack in a baking tin so it is not resting in the hot fat and never use the fat to make sauces or gravy. Skim off the fat, which will be floating on top of the meat juices, then use those juices in sauces. Mince frequently contains a very high proportion of fat so, if possible, either buy lean meat and mince it yourself or, if shopping in a supermarket, buy packaged mince labelled 'extra lean' or 'low-fat'.

Before including meat other than poultry or offal in any recipe, apart from baking or roasting, prepare in the following way: place on a rack under the grill or in a moderately hot oven and heat for a few minutes until the fat stops dripping or place in cold water and bring to the boil, then cool rapidly and skim off the fat. Minced meat must be formed into small patties before grilling.

All weights listed in the recipe ingredients are for uncooked but trimmed weight. As there is some weight loss during cooking (4oz/120g is reduced to about 3oz/90g), Protein Selections and calorie counts are calculated after cooking.

FISH

Buy only really fresh fish which is unblemished, shiny and bright-eyed.

The weight of cooked fish free from bones is often considerably less than the purchase weight of whole fish, steaks, cutlets or even fillets. As a very rough guide, ½oz (15g) of bone is contained in a steak or fillet and there is approximately 1oz (30g) weight loss in every 4oz (120g) of fish flesh.

CHEESE

There is a huge range of cheese available now but many are very high in fat and therefore in calories. Low-fat soft cheeses containing no more than 50 Calories per ounce (30g), or 180 Calories per 100g (3½ oz) include fromage frais (the 1% and 8% fat varieties), quark, cottage cheese and most curd cheeses. Hard cheeses such as Cheddar, Gorgonzola and Emmental, which contain up to 120 Calories per ounce (30g) are included in many recipes but varieties higher in fat, such as Blue Stilton and Norwegian Giest, should be avoided. Very little cream cheese is used in the recipes as it is extremely high in calories.

TOFU AND TEMPEH

Only a few years ago tofu and tempeh were regarded as purely vegetarian foods but nowadays they are included in many non-vegetarian recipes.

Tofu is a low-fat curd made from the soya bean. It does not require cooking but is used in many cooked dishes. There are several varieties on sale: some fresh, others canned or prepacked long-life. These include plain, marinated, smoked and braised.

Tempeh is a fermented bean curd which must be cooked, either by steaming or stir-frying. Many healthfood shops sell frozen tempeh.

EGGS

Unless otherwise stated, always use size 3.

MILK

Always use fresh, long-life or powdered reconstituted skimmed milk unless you are following recipes which list 'whole milk' in the ingredients. Sometimes fresh milk is necessary – for example when making junket. Occasionally dried skimmed milk is preferable, for example when making yogurt. Buttermilk can be used in some recipes such as scones or milkshakes.

FATS AND OILS

The recipes in this book include oils, polyunsaturated margarines, low-fat spreads, mayonnaise and salad dressings in restricted quantities. Polyunsaturated margarines tend to be soft; store small amounts in the freezer so they are firmer and can be more easily incorporated in recipes such as crumble toppings which use the 'rubbing in' method.

When a recipe lists 'vegetable oil' or just 'oil' it is advisable to use a specific oil, for example, safflower, soya or corn oils. Bottles of vegetable oil contain many different blends. Some oils, such as olive and sesame, have a strong distinct flavour which is preferable for salad dressings. Olive oil should not be used for stir-frying or when cooking to a high temperature as it burns at a lower temperature than many other oils.

The quantity of fat and oil, and consequently calories, can be reduced by using non-stick baking parchment to line cake tins, baking sheets etc. in place of greasing.

Low-fat spreads have a high water content and are therefore not suitable for cooking.

FRUIT AND VEGETABLES

Good-quality fruit and vegetables are available throughout the year. To enjoy them at their best either eat them raw or cook them for a short time in as little liquid as possible. If you can, use their cooking liquid in accompanying sauces. Whenever possible avoid peeling, just make sure they're well washed and prepare them immediately prior to cooking. If it isn't possible to use fresh produce substitute frozen, canned or dried. Never use fruits or vegetables with added sugar and weigh the canned varieties well-drained.

SEASONINGS

A bland recipe can be transformed to a tasty, appetising dish by the use of seasonings. Herbs, spices, Worcestershire and soy sauce are just a few of the ingredients which give dishes an improved flavour.

If possible use fresh herbs and substitute listed quantities of dried with about three times the quantity of fresh. Dried herbs and spices lose their flavour during storage. To minimise this, always store them in airtight containers in a cool dark cupboard. Never keep them longer than one year.

SWEETENERS

Several recipes are sweetened with sugar and honey, but if you prefer a sweeter flavour add artificial sweetener whenever appropriate. Study the labelling of sweeteners carefully as some are not suitable for cooking.

WEIGHING

Accuracy is vital to successful cooking and your own weight loss. Measure all ingredients carefully and use either the imperial or metric system – never mix the two. One teaspoon is equivalent to 5ml, one tablespoon is equal to 15ml. All spoon measurements should be level.

VEGETARIANS

As vegetarians do not eat meat or fish some recipes have been included especially for them. These recipes include ingredients such as nuts, which are high in protein and fat and therefore are only suitable for those who have excluded meat and fish from their diet. Recipes devised exclusively for vegetarians are indicated by the symbol ● .

There are many recipes which are suitable for the vegetarian as well as the non-vegetarian since, if an ingredient such as gelatine is listed, it is frequently possible to substitute a vegetable-based gelling agent. Recipes suitable for vegetarians as well as non-vegetarians are indicated in each chapter contents list by *.

Ice Cream Cake (page 120)

COOKING ON A SHOESTRING

Cooking on a limited budget needn't mean you have to eat poor-quality bland meals. In fact, by choosing seasonal fruits and vegetables when they are in plentiful supply money is saved and tasty produce is assured. Many of the cheaper cuts of meat, such as scrag of lamb and chuck steak, have more flavour than the more expensive tender cuts but they require long, moist methods of cooking to break down their coarse fibres. When cooking meat by these methods it is advisable to bring to the boil slowly then skim off any fat which rises to the surface, instead of pre-grilling so the fat drips from the meat.

Considerable savings can be made by preparing fish, meat and (for vegetarians) nuts yourself instead of buying them ready-prepared. For example, it is more economical to purchase a whole fish and fillet it yourself than to buy fish fillets from a supermarket. Nuts can be bought in their shells and the shell removed at home, or nuts such as almonds can be purchased in their skins, covered with boiling water and the skins slipped off. This is far cheaper than purchasing blanched almonds. These processes take time but, with practice, save considerable amounts of money.

If you are particularly fond of herbs try growing them yourself in a garden, window box or as a household pot plant. They can then be used fresh, dried or frozen. To freeze: place a bunch of herbs in a bag, freeze, crush the bag to break up the herbs, then replace in the freezer. This saves chopping. Either dry herbs in bunches in a warm, dry atmosphere or, if you have a microwave oven, follow the manufacturer's instructions and speed up this process.

Instead of spending money on specialised kitchen equipment make full use of what you already have. If a recipe says to use a wok, cook in a frying pan or saucepan. If the instructions say 'liquidise' or 'process in a food processor', finely chop or sieve the food, whichever is appropriate. The end result may not have the same texture but the flavour should be retained. A pressure cooker cuts down cooking time and therefore saves fuel. A steamer can be used to cook vegetables while meat or fish is cooked in the saucepan beneath it. If you don't own a steamer substitute a heat-proof colander or sieve. A plate can be rested on a saucepan containing one recipe which requires simmering, and fish fillets can be laid on the plate, then covered and steamed over the saucepan. When a recipe requires long slow cooking, for example a casserole, either cook it in an oven with another recipe such as a milk pudding or place it in a heavy-based saucepan, cover and place over a very low heat so it barely simmers. Cooking on the hob is much cheaper than heating and cooking in an oven.

All recipes marked * are suitable for vegetarians as well as non-vegetarians

SAVOURY RICE

SERVES 2

450 CALORIES PER SERVING

The nutty flavour of the basmati rice is ideal for this dish.

4oz (120g) brown basmati rice

2 teaspoons oil, preferably walnut oil

I clove garlic, chopped

I onion, chopped

stock or water

Ioz (30g) cashew nuts, roughly chopped

2oz (60g) Cheddar cheese, grated

salt

chopped parsley

Tip:
Look out in shops for broken cashew kernels – they can be much cheaper than the whole ones.

1. Soak the rice in plenty of water for 15 minutes then drain.
2. Heat the oil in a saucepan, add the garlic and onion and stir-fry for about 4 minutes. Stir in the rice and twice the rice's volume of stock or water. Cook according to the packaging instructions until the rice is cooked and the liquid has been absorbed.
3. Remove from the heat and stir in the cashew nuts and cheese. Season with a little salt, spoon onto a warm serving dish, sprinkle with the chopped parsley, then serve.

Selections per serving:
  2 Bread
  1 ½ Fat
  2 Protein
  ½ Vegetable
  5 Optional Calories

CANNELLONI

SERVES 3

465 CALORIES PER SERVING

Mushroom ketchup is available in most super-markets and delicatessens.

12oz (360g) minced beef

1½ teaspoons margarine

3oz (90g) mushrooms, finely chopped

1oz (30g) cornflour

½ pint (300ml) skimmed milk

1 teaspoon mushroom ketchup

1½ teaspoons oil

1 large onion, thinly sliced

1 tablespoon flour

4fl oz (120ml) tomato and vegetable juice

1 medium (15oz/497g) can chopped tomatoes

1 tablespoon finely chopped basil

4oz (120g) cannelloni (12 tubes)

Tip:
If you are unable to buy cannelloni substitute with the same weight of lasagne. Halve the sheets of lasagne and roll round the stuffing. Secure with cocktail sticks and bake as above.

1. Shape the minced beef into six patties, place on the rack of a grill pan and grill, turning once, until cooked.
2. Heat the margarine in a small saucepan, add the mushrooms and stir-fry for 2–3 minutes. Then reduce the heat and leave the mushrooms to simmer in their own juice for 6–7 minutes until the liquid has evaporated.
3. Blend the cornflour with the milk, stir into the mushrooms and bring to the boil, stirring all the time. Boil for 1 minute until very thick. Stir in the mushroom ketchup and crumble in the cooked minced beef.
4. Heat the oil in a separate saucepan, add the onion and stir-fry for 4–5 minutes until the onion is limp. Sprinkle in the flour, stir well, then gradually add the tomato and vegetable juice. Add the chopped tomatoes and basil. Bring to the boil, stirring all the time. Reduce the heat and simmer for 5 minutes.
5. Pack the beef and mushroom filling into the cannelloni.
6. Spread a thin layer of the tomato and onion sauce over a long thin ovenproof dish. Lay the stuffed cannelloni in a single layer in the dish and pour over the remaining sauce.
7. Bake the Cannelloni at 400°F, 200°C, Gas Mark 6 for 30 minutes.

Selections per serving:
1½ Bread
1 Fat
¼ Milk
3 Protein
2 Vegetable
45 Optional Calories

BITS AND PIECES

SERVES 4

40 CALORIES PER SERVING

Use this recipe as a guide; it is a good way of incorporating small amounts of vegetables left over from other recipes, for example replace the leek with a large onion, the cabbage with frozen peas. It's very adaptable!

1 small onion, diced

1 leek, diced

8oz (240g) mixture of carrots, celery, swede, diced

2 tablespoons tomato purée

1½ pints (900ml) vegetable stock

2 tablespoons chopped parsley

salt and pepper

3oz (90g) cauliflower or broccoli florets

3oz (90g) cabbage, shredded

Tip:
Serve with crusty rolls or French bread.

1. Place the onion, leek, carrot mixture, tomato purée, stock, parsley and a little salt and pepper in a saucepan. Bring to the boil, reduce the heat, cover and simmer for 20 minutes.
2. Cut the cauliflower or broccoli into very tiny florets.
3. Add the florets and cabbage to the saucepan and simmer for 10 minutes.
4. Ladle into four warm bowls.

Selections per serving:
   1½ Vegetable
   10 Optional Calories

CURRIED MINCE

SERVES 4

290 CALORIES PER SERVING

This curry requires long, slow cooking. If you don't want to have the oven on for such a long time it can be cooked on the hob, but use a very low heat, stir occasionally and if necessary add more water.

1lb 4oz (600g) minced beef

2 teaspoons oil

1 clove garlic, chopped

1 onion, chopped

1 tablespoon hot Madras curry powder

1 medium apple, grated or chopped

3oz (90g) carrot, grated

1 small (8oz/227g) can chopped tomatoes

4 tablespoons water

5fl oz (150ml) low-fat natural yogurt

Tip:
It is often more economical to mince your own beef.

1. Form the minced beef into patties, place on the rack of a grill pan and grill, turning once, until the fat stops dripping from the meat.
2. Heat the oil in a flameproof casserole. Add the garlic and onion and stir-fry for 3–4 minutes.
3. Stir the curry powder into the casserole then mix in the apple, carrot, tomatoes, water and yogurt. Crumble the minced beef into the casserole and slowly bring to the boil.
4. Cover the casserole dish and transfer to the oven set at 325°F, 160°C, Gas Mark 3 for 1½ hours.

Selections per serving:
½ Fat
¼ Fruit
¼ Milk
4 Protein
1 Vegetable

BEEF CASSEROLE

SERVES 4

340 CALORIES PER SERVING

Chuck steak is a very economical cut of beef which is full of flavour, however it requires long slow cooking to make it really tender. For this reason it is preferable to bring the beef to the boil and skim off the fat rather than grilling to remove fat.

1lb 4oz (600g) chuck steak

3 large leeks

8oz (240g) carrots

2 tomatoes

9oz (270g) drained canned sweetcorn

4 teaspoons cornflour

¾ pint (450ml) beef stock

salt and pepper

Tip:
Make full use of the lengthy cooking time and bake a dessert, for example baked apples or a vegetable such as jacket potatoes, at the same time.

1. Cut the precooked meat into cubes.
2. Cut the leeks into 2-inch (5-cm) slices. Cut the carrots into chunks. Cover the tomatoes with boiling water, leave for 30 seconds, then slip off the tomato skins. Quarter the tomatoes.
3. Place the beef and vegetables in an ovenproof dish.
4. Blend the cornflour with the stock and pour into the dish. Season with a little salt and pepper, cover and cook at 325°F, 160°C, Gas Mark 3 for 2½ hours. Stir two or three times during cooking.

Selections per serving:
  ¾ Bread
  4 Protein
  2 Vegetable
  10 Optional Calories

BEEF HOT POT

SERVES 6

280 CALORIES PER SERVING

As the hot pot is cooked in the oven for so long, I suggest you either make double the quantity and freeze half or cook a dessert at the same time.

1 aubergine

salt

1lb 8oz (720g) braising steak

1 medium (15oz/497g) can chopped tomatoes

3 sticks celery

1 red pepper

1lb 2oz (540g) potatoes

¼ pint (150ml) stock

1oz (30g) Cheddar cheese, grated

Tip:
Prepare and cook Bread Pudding (p.36) at the same time. Both recipes are cooked at 325°F, 160°C, Gas Mark 3.

1. Cut the aubergine into six thick slices, place in a sieve or colander and sprinkle with salt. Leave for 20–30 minutes then rinse well.
2. Lay the beef on the rack of a grill pan, grill under a moderate heat, turning once, until the fat stops dripping.
3. Cut the beef into large chunks. Place half the beef in an ovenproof dish with the aubergine and tomatoes.
4. Cut the celery into 3-inch (7.5-cm) lengths. Remove the seeds from the pepper and cut into 1-inch (2.5-cm) squares. Add half the celery and pepper to the dish.
5. Cut the potatoes into thin slices. Arrange about a third of them on top of the vegetables then add the remaining beef, vegetables, celery and pepper.
6. Arrange the remaining potato with slices overlapping on top. Pour the stock over, cover the dish and bake at 325°F, 160°C, Gas Mark 3 for 2¼ hours. Remove the lid, sprinkle with the cheese and grill for a few minutes until bubbling and golden brown.

Selections per serving:
 1 Bread
 3½ Protein
 1¾ Vegetable

FISH PIE

SERVES 4

320 CALORIES PER SERVING

Coley is a cheap fish which can be used successfully in a well-flavoured dish but, when money allows, treat yourself to cod or haddock.

1lb 8oz (720g) potatoes

salt

2 tablespoons skimmed milk

2 teaspoons oil

1 clove garlic, chopped

1 onion, thinly sliced

1 small green pepper, seeded, halved and sliced

1–1½ teaspoons mild chilli powder

1 tablespoon flour

1 medium (15oz/497g) can chopped tomatoes

2–3 tablespoons water or stock

1lb (480g) coley, haddock or cod

2oz (60g) prawns

2 teaspoons margarine

Tip:
Serve with garden peas and carrots.

1. Cut the potatoes into large pieces, boil in salted water until tender. Drain and mash with the milk.
2. Heat the oil in a saucepan, add the garlic and onion and stir-fry for 3–4 minutes. Add the green pepper and stir-fry for a further 3 minutes.
3. Stir the chilli powder and flour into the saucepan. Gradually add the tomatoes and 2 tablespoons water or stock. Bring to the boil, stirring all the time.
4. Remove the skin from the fish and cut into 2-inch (2.5-cm) squares. Lay the fish on top of the vegetables, partially cover the saucepan and simmer for 8 minutes. If necessary add another tablespoon of water or stock.
5. Stir the prawns into the fish and vegetables then spoon into an ovenproof dish.
6. Spoon the hot mashed potato on top of the fish and roughen the surface with a fork. Dot the margarine over the potato and bake at 375°F, 190°C, Gas Mark 5 for 20 minutes. Transfer to a hot grill to brown the potato.

Selections per serving:
2 Bread
1 Fat
4 Protein
1½ Vegetables
10 Optional Calories

STUFFED MACKEREL

SERVES 4

220 CALORIES PER SERVING

This recipe requires whole, not filleted mackerel. To obtain the required weight choose a fish weighing about 6oz (180g) and ask the fishmonger to clean it and remove the head, tail and central bone.

4 × 4½oz (135g) cleaned and boned mackerel

1oz (30g) watercress

2oz (60g) breadcrumbs

1 medium orange

4 tablespoons water

Tip:
It is usually more economical to buy a bunch of watercress from a greengrocer than a pre-packed selection of sprigs of watercress from a supermarket.

1. Lay the mackerel flat, skin side down.
2. Roughly chop the watercress and mix with the breadcrumbs.
3. Cut the orange in half. Cut the peel and pith from half of the orange and chop into large pieces.
4. Mix the orange with the watercress and breadcrumbs – the stuffing will not bind well but do not add additional liquid.
5. Spoon the stuffing over half of each mackerel then fold over and transfer to an ovenproof dish. Add the water then cover with foil and bake at 350°F, 180°C, Gas Mark 4 for 25–30 minutes.
6. Using a fish slice carefully remove the mackerel from the dish. Cut the reserved orange half into four wedges and garnish each Stuffed Mackerel with an orange wedge.

Selections per serving:
½ Bread
¼ Fruit
3½ Protein

25

SPICY BEANS

SERVES 4

235 CALORIES PER SERVING

This recipe can be made in advance and heated up in the oven or on the hob.

8oz (240g) mixture of dried beans e.g. red and white kidney, butter, haricot

1 tablespoon oil

8oz (240g) leeks, sliced

2 sticks celery and their leaves, chopped

4oz (120g) carrot, grated

2 medium (15oz/497g) cans chopped tomatoes

1 tablespoon ground coriander

1 tablespoon ground cinnamon

salt and pepper

Tip:
Don't add any salt when cooking the beans or the skins may harden.

1. Place the beans in a bowl, cover with plenty of cold water and leave to soak for several hours or overnight.
2. Drain the beans, cover with fresh cold water and bring to the boil over a moderate heat. Boil rapidly for 10 minutes then reduce the heat, cover the saucepan and boil for 30 minutes.
3. Heat the oil in a saucepan, add the leeks and stir-fry for 1 minute. Cover the saucepan and leave the leeks over a low heat for 5 minutes.
4. Stir the celery, carrot, tomatoes and spices into the leeks.
5. Drain the beans then stir into the tomato mixture. Bring to the boil and simmer for 30 minutes. Season well, then serve.

Selections per serving:
¾ Fat
2 Protein
3 Vegetable

LIVER AND BEANS

SERVES 4

425 CALORIES PER SERVING

This filling meal can be made in half an hour. While the liver is simmering prepare and cook a green vegetable to serve with it.

2 teaspoons oil

2 onions, halved and sliced

1 green pepper, halved, seeded and sliced

1lb (480g) lamb's liver

15oz (450g) can baked beans

3oz (90g) pasta shapes

½ pint (300ml) stock

1 tablespoon Worcestershire sauce

2 tablespoons vinegar

good pinch of mixed herbs

5fl oz (150ml) low-fat natural yogurt

Tip:
To keep the calorie count as low as possible use reduced-calorie baked beans.

1. Heat the oil in a saucepan and stir-fry the onion for 1 minute. Add the pepper and place the lid on the saucepan. Leave over a low heat for 3–4 minutes.
2. Cut the liver into strips. Stir the liver, beans, pasta, stock, Worcestershire sauce, vinegar and herbs into the saucepan, cover and leave to simmer for 15–20 minutes until cooked. Stir the mixture occasionally to prevent it sticking to the bottom of the saucepan.
3. Remove the saucepan from the heat, stir in the yogurt and serve.

Selections per serving:
  2 Bread
  ½ Fat
  ¼ Milk
  3½ Protein
  ¾ Vegetable

HEARTY LAMB STEW

SERVES 4

365 CALORIES PER SERVING

There is a considerable amount of bone and fat on scrag of lamb but it has a lot of flavour. Buy just over 2lbs (960g) then, when you have trimmed off the fat, there should be sufficient for this stew.

1lb 12oz (840g) scrag of lamb, cut into eight pieces

1 pint (600ml) stock

1 large onion

8oz (240g) parsnip

8oz (240g) swede

1 medium (14oz/400g) can whole tomatoes

2oz (60g) pearl barley

large sprig of mint

Tip:
To maintain a round-the-year supply of mint, dig up a root of mint during the summer, transfer it to a flowerpot and keep in the house throughout the winter.

1. Place the lamb and stock in a saucepan over a very low heat and slowly bring to the boil. Simmer gently for 3–4 minutes then cool rapidly and skim off the fat.
2. Chop the onion. Cut the parsnip and swede into 1-inch (2.5-cm) cubes.
3. Mix the lamb, stock, vegetables, pearl barley and mint in a casserole dish. Transfer to an oven and cook at 325°F, 160°C, Gas Mark 3 for 2½ hours.

Selections per serving:
½ Bread
2¾ Protein
3 Vegetable

PORK WITH LENTILS

SERVES 4

240 CALORIES PER SERVING

Keep the saucepan covered throughout the cooking time to prevent burning.

1lb (480g) lean pork

2oz (60g) split lentils

4fl oz (120ml) vegetable stock

8fl oz (240ml) vegetable juice

1oz (30g) watercress

1 stick celery

2 leeks

1 carrot

salt and pepper

Tip:
Never add salt when cooking pulses – it will harden the skins.

1. Lay the pork on the rack of a grill pan, grill under a moderate heat, turning once, until the fat stops dripping.
2. Place the lentils in a saucepan, add the vegetable stock and juice.
3. Cut the pork into 1-inch (2.5-cm) pieces and stir into the saucepan.
4. Wash the watercress well and finely chop the leaves and stems. Chop the celery, leeks and carrot.
5. Stir all the prepared vegetables into the saucepan and place over a low heat. Bring to the boil, stir well, cover and leave to simmer for 30 minutes, stirring occasionally. Season well with salt and pepper.

Selections per serving:
  1/2 Bread
  1/4 Fruit
  3 1/2 Protein
  1 Vegetable

VEGETABLE LASAGNE

SERVES 6

365 CALORIES PER SERVING

The precooked lasagne is more expensive than the type I have suggested which requires boiling; however if you choose to use the precooked variety, add 3 tablespoons water to the spinach mixture.

2lbs (960g) spinach

2 teaspoons oil

I clove garlic, finely chopped

I onion, finely chopped

I small red pepper, seeded and finely chopped

2 tablespoons tomato purée

9oz (270g) smoked tofu, grated

6oz (180g) lasagne (9 sheets)

salt

2oz (60g) cornflour

I¼ pints (750ml) skimmed milk

4½oz (135g) cheese, grated

I teaspoon margarine

Tip:
Try the wholemeal or green varieties of lasagne for a change.

1. Wash the spinach in several changes of water. Shake excess water from the leaves and place in a large saucepan. Cover and cook over a low heat until the spinach is tender – about 6–7 minutes. Drain well, leave to cool then squeeze to remove as much moisture as possible. Roughly chop the leaves.
2. Heat the oil in a saucepan. Add the garlic, onion and red pepper and stir-fry for 2–3 minutes. Remove from the heat and stir in the spinach, tomato purée and tofu.
3. Boil the lasagne in salted water until just cooked and drain well.
4. While the lasagne is cooking, blend the cornflour and milk together. Bring to the boil, stirring all the time, and simmer for 1–2 minutes. Stir a little less than ½ pint (300ml) of the sauce into the spinach and tofu.
5. Reserve 1oz (30g) cheese, add the remainder to the white sauce and stir until melted.
6. Grease a dish just large enough to hold three sheets of lasagne side by side with the margarine.
7. Spread a thin layer of cheese sauce over the base of the dish. Lay three sheets of lasagne on top, then spread half the spinach and tofu on top of the lasagne. Cover with three more sheets of pasta then the remaining spinach and tofu. Arrange the remaining lasagne and spread the remaining cheese sauce over the top. Sprinkle with the reserved cheese and bake at 375°F, 190°C, Gas Mark 5 for 30 minutes. Brown under a hot grill.

Selections per serving:
I¼ Bread
½ Fat
¼ Milk
I¼ Protein
I¼ Vegetable
25 Optional Calories

Vegetable Lasagne

SUMMERTIME CHICKEN

SERVES 2

275 CALORIES PER SERVING

This recipe is very economical during the summer months when tomatoes are cheap, basil is available and spring onions have come down in price.

2 × 8oz (240g) chicken leg quarters

2 teaspoons oil

4 bulbous spring onions, chopped

12oz (360g) tomatoes, skinned and chopped

1 tablespoon chopped basil

4fl oz (120ml) chicken or vegetable stock

Tip:
Tomatoes may be frozen whole then used in casseroles or stews (they would not be suitable for salads after freezing).

1. Remove the chicken skin and the white fat just below the skin – this is most easily done by holding the chicken with a piece of kitchen paper.
2. Heat the oil in a saucepan just large enough to hold the chicken. Turn the chicken in the oil then transfer to a plate and add the onions and tomatoes to the saucepan. Add the basil and stock and bring to the boil.
3. Turn the heat as low as possible, lay the chicken on the tomatoes, cover the saucepan and leave to barely simmer for 30–35 minutes or until the chicken is cooked.
4. Lift the chicken out of the saucepan and keep warm while completing the tomato sauce. Boil the tomato and stock mixture fiercely until reduced to a thick sauce, pour over the chicken and serve.

Selections per serving:
1 Fat
4 Protein
2 Vegetable

TANDOORI CHICKEN

SERVES 4

170 CALORIES PER SERVING

This makes an economical recipe suitable for entertaining.

5fl oz (150ml) low-fat natural yogurt

½ teaspoon ground ginger

1 teaspoon ground coriander

1 teaspoon ground cumin

½–¾ teaspoon hot chilli powder

¼ teaspoon turmeric

1 clove garlic

4 × 4½oz (135g) boneless, skinned chicken breasts

¼ teaspoon oil

Tip:
This recipe may be cooked on a barbecue.

1. Stir the yogurt, ginger, coriander, cumin, chilli powder and turmeric together. Crush the garlic and stir into the spiced yogurt.
2. Turn the chicken breasts in the spiced marinade and lay on a plate, but make sure the side which is facing the plate is well coated. Spoon over any remaining marinade and place in the refrigerator for 4–6 hours or overnight.
3. Brush the rack of the grill pan with the oil. Transfer the chicken to the grill pan. Cook about 2 inches (5cm) below the heat for about 15 minutes, turning once, until cooked.

Selections per serving:
¼ Milk
3½ Protein
5 Optional Calories

BREAD AND BUTTER PUDDING

SERVES 4

260 CALORIES PER SERVING

Although margarine high in polyunsaturates is recommended for an everyday spread and for cooking, butter gives a rich creamy flavour to this simple tasty pudding.

4oz (120g) bread, thinly sliced

2 tablespoons butter

3oz (90g) mixed dried fruit

1½ tablespoons caster sugar

2 eggs

½ pint (300ml) skimmed milk

good pinch of mixed spice

Tip:
If you are in a hurry, the standing time may be omitted but the texture will not be the same.

1. Spread the bread with the butter then cut each slice into four triangles.
2. Arrange half the bread butterside uppermost in a 1½-pint (900-ml) ovenproof dish, sprinkle half the mixed fruit and sugar over the top.
3. Arrange the remaining bread and butter, butterside uppermost, on top of the mixed fruit then sprinkle with the remaining fruit and sugar.
4. Whisk the eggs together with the milk and mixed spice, pour over the bread and leave for 20–30 minutes.
5. Bake at 350°F, 180°C, Gas Mark 4 for 30–40 minutes until golden and puffy.

Selections per serving:
1 Bread
¾ Fruit
½ Protein
¼ Milk
75 Optional Calories

Bread and Butter Pudding

BREAD PUDDING

SERVES 4

200 CALORIES PER SERVING

This pudding isn't like the traditional heavy pudding made with suet – it is much lighter.

½ teaspoon margarine

4oz (120g) crustless wholemeal bread, 2–3 days old

¼ pint (150ml) skimmed milk

1 egg

finely grated zest of ½ an orange

1 tablespoon orange juice

1 tablespoon soft brown sugar

½–1 teaspoon mixed spice

3 tablespoons low-fat spread, melted

2oz (60g) dried fruit

½ teaspoon caster sugar

Tip:
Cook in the same oven as Beef Hot Pot (p.22) which is cooked at the same temperature.

1. Grease a 6-inch (15-cm) shallow dish or tin with the margarine.
2. Tear the bread into small pieces and place in a bowl.
3. Whisk 1–2 tablespoons milk with the egg and put to one side. Pour the remaining milk over the bread and leave for 30 minutes.
4. Beat the bread until smooth then beat in all the remaining ingredients except the caster sugar. Spoon the mixture into the greased dish and bake at 325°F, 160°C, Gas Mark 3 for 1½–1¾ hours. Remove from the oven and sprinkle with caster sugar. Cut into squares and serve hot or cold.

Selections per serving:
  1 Bread
  1¼ Fat
  ½ Fruit
  ¼ Protein
  30 Optional Calories

APRICOT CUSTARD

SERVES 4

95 CALORIES PER SERVING

This recipe can be adapted to suit your taste or whichever fruit is in the store cupboard. Always drain the fruit very well.

8oz (240g) drained canned apricots

4oz (120g) quark

1 egg, beaten

1 tablespoon caster sugar

few drops of almond essence

¼ pint (150ml) skimmed milk

Tip:
Always stand baked egg custards in a bath of hot water to help prevent the eggs curdling.

1. Chop the apricots and divide between four ramekins, spreading them evenly over the base.
2. Spoon the quark into a bowl, gradually add the beaten egg, then stir in the sugar and almond essence.
3. Heat the milk until steaming then gradually add to the quark mixture. Spoon the milk and quark over the chopped apricots in each ramekin.
4. Stand the ramekins in a roasting tin and add hot water to the tin until the ramekins stand in about ½ inch (1.25cm) of water. Transfer to an oven and cook at 375°F, 160°C, Gas Mark 3 for 25–30 minutes until set.
5. Remove the Apricot Custard from the water bath and serve warm, or chill until cold before serving.

Selections per serving:
½ Fruit
¾ Protein
30 Optional Calories

BERRY JELLY

SERVES 4

105 CALORIES PER SERVING

Make this recipe in late summer when the raspberries are still available and the blackberries are just ripe.

4fl oz (120ml) apple juice

4½ teaspoons gelatine

6oz (180g) strawberries

3oz (90g) raspberries

3oz (90g) blackberries

3oz (90g) blueberries

4 teaspoons caster sugar

8oz (240g) fromage frais

Tip:
If entertaining, decorate the jelly with tiny leaves from the berry plants or bushes.

1. Spoon 3 tablespoons of apple juice into a cup or small bowl, sprinkle in the gelatine and stir well. Stand the cup in a saucepan of simmering water until dissolved.
2. Place the remaining apple juice in a blender and add the strawberries, raspberries, blackberries and blueberries. Process for a few seconds, then add the sugar and 6oz (180g) fromage frais and process once again.
3. Strain the fruit purée through a sieve, pressing the mixture until only the pips remain.
4. Stir the dissolved gelatine into the fruit purée and leave until just set. Whisk the setting jelly until foaming. Divide the jelly between four serving glasses or dishes and chill until set.
5. Spoon the remaining fromage frais on top of the jelly before serving.

Selections per serving:
   1 Fruit
   1 Protein
   20 Optional Calories

FRUIT DIP

SERVES 2

205 CALORIES PER SERVING

This delicious chocolate dip costs very little. The low-fat fromage frais is cheaper than the higher fat variety and by using seasonal fruits the cost is kept down. Increase the quantities and this can be served at dinner parties for any number of guests.

1oz (30g) plain chocolate

1½ teaspoons golden syrup

6oz (180g) fromage frais

4oz (120g) mixture of fresh or well-drained canned pineapple and apricots

1 kiwi fruit

5oz (150g) strawberries

Tip:
For a dinner party reserve 1 teaspoon fromage frais and swirl into the chocolate dip just before serving.

1. Break the chocolate into a small basin and stand in a saucepan of simmering water until melted.
2. Stir the chocolate, add the syrup and a little fromage frais and stir again. The chocolate will be very stiff but stand the basin back in the saucepan and the mixture will become smooth once again. Continue until all the fromage frais has been added. Leave to cool.
3. Cut the pineapple in chunks. Halve and remove the stones from the apricots, then cut into quarters.
4. Cut the kiwi fruit into six or eight segments, not slices.
5. Leave small strawberries whole but cut large ones in half.
6. Spoon the chocolate mixture into two small dishes, and surround them with the prepared fruits. Serve with cocktail sticks so the fruit can easily be dipped into the chocolate sauce then eaten.

Selections per serving:
1½ Fruit
1½ Protein
90 Optional Calories

FRUIT RICE PUDDING

SERVES 4

190 CALORIES PER SERVING

This recipe uses whole milk, not skimmed, so the pudding has a richer, creamier flavour.

2oz (60g) mixture of dried fruits e.g. sultanas, raisins, apricots

finely grated zest and juice of 1 medium orange

1½oz (45g) ground rice

1 pint (600ml) whole milk

1½ tablespoons sugar

Tip:
Flaked rice may be used in place of the ground rice.

1. Place the sultanas and raisins in a small bowl. If using apricots or larger dried fruit chop into small pieces and add to the basin. Pour the orange juice over the fruit and leave for several hours or overnight.
2. Place the ground rice in a small saucepan and gradually blend in the milk. Add the fruit, remaining orange juice, zest and sugar.
3. Bring the milk to the boil, stirring all the time. Reduce the heat and allow the pudding to simmer very gently for 10 minutes until thick. Continue stirring the mixture with a wooden spoon or the milk will stick to the saucepan and burn.
4. Pour the pudding into four warm serving dishes.

Selections per serving:
¼ Bread
¾ Fruit
1 Milk
80 Optional Calories

STRAWBERRY MOUSSE DESSERT

SERVES 2

175 CALORIES PER SERVING

Don't make this dessert more than two hours in advance or the egg white will start to separate.

5oz (150g) strawberries

1 tablespoon caster sugar

6oz (180g) low fat soft cheese

1 egg white

pinch of cream of tartar

Tip:
Make this dessert during the summer when strawberries are plentiful, cheap and full of flavour.

1. Place the strawberries, sugar and soft cheese in a blender and process until smooth.
2. Whisk the egg white and cream of tartar until peaking.
3. Fold the egg white into the strawberry cheese purée.
4. Spoon the mousse into two serving glasses or dishes and chill before serving.

Selections per serving:
½ Fruit
1½ Protein
40 Optional Calories

RASPBERRY AND VANILLA DESSERT

SERVES 4

120 CALORIES PER SERVING

Fresh or frozen raspberries may be used for this dessert but if you prefer, substitute with the same weight of strawberries.

8oz (240g) cottage cheese

5fl oz (150ml) low-fat natural yogurt

4 teaspoons caster sugar

½ teaspoon vanilla essence

I tablespoon lemon juice

I tablespoon water

I tablespoon gelatine

5oz (150g) raspberries

¼oz (10g) plain chocolate, grated

Tip:
If you wish to make this recipe for a vegetarian, substitute the gelatine with a vegetable gelling agent.

1. Place the cottage cheese, yogurt, sugar and vanilla essence in a food processor or blender. Process until smooth and then pour into a bowl.
2. Pour the lemon juice and water in a small basin or cup. Sprinkle the gelatine into the liquid, stir, then stand the basin in a saucepan of simmering water until dissolved.
3. Stir the dissolved gelatine into the cheese and yogurt mixture and leave until beginning to set.
4. Divide the raspberries between four serving glasses. Spoon the setting cheese mixture on top of the fruit and chill until set. Decorate each dessert with the grated chocolate.

Selections per serving:
¼ Fruit
¼ Milk
I Protein
30 Optional Calories

SWEET COTTAGE CRÊPES

SERVES 6

215 CALORIES PER SERVING

Before cooking the crêpes prove the griddle or frying pan well. Heat a little salt in it, rub round with kitchen paper, tip the salt out and rub well once again.

6oz (180g) self-raising flour

4oz (120g) cottage cheese

¼ pint (150ml) buttermilk

5 teaspoons caster sugar

2 eggs

finely grated zest of ½ a lemon

1 tablespoon oil

3 tablespoons jam

½–1 teaspoon lemon juice

Tip:
If the jam contains large pieces of fruit, either mash with a fork to break them up or sieve before measuring the 3 tablespoons of jam required.

1. Sieve the flour into a bowl. Sieve the cottage cheese and stir in the buttermilk.
2. Make a well in the centre of the flour. Add the sugar, eggs and lemon zest. Gradually add the buttermilk and cheese, beating well so the batter is smooth. Alternatively place all the ingredients in a liquidiser or food processor and process until smooth.
3. Heat a little oil in the griddle or large frying pan. Tip the pan so the oil just coats the base. Spoon a little of the batter into the pan, to form about a 3-inch (7.5-cm) crêpe. Add more batter so three or four crêpes are cooked at the same time.
4. Cook over a moderate heat until the top of each crêpe begins to set and the base is lightly golden. Using a palette knife turn over and cook the underside.
5. Transfer the crêpes to a plate and keep warm in a low oven while cooking the remaining batter. The mixture will make twelve crêpes.
6. Place the jam and lemon juice in a small saucepan and heat gently until the jam has melted.
7. Transfer two crêpes to each serving plate, spoon over a little of the jam sauce and serve.

Selections per serving:
　1 Bread
　½ Fat
　½ Protein
　65 Optional Calories.

COLD
CONCOCTIONS

Recipes which can be made in advance and retain their flavour and texture are invaluable. A prepared cold dish saves turning on the oven or hob during a hot summer's day, is ideal for a hurried meal or when there is little time for cooking and enables the host or hostess to relax with guests knowing the food is all ready.

So often when arriving home tired from work or a shopping expedition the thought of preparing and cooking a meal is just too much. It is at these times inadequate snacks, which do very little to satisfy hunger for more than one or two hours, are very tempting and after you have eaten one the desire to nibble returns. When you know in advance you will be tired I suggest the preparation and cooking is carried out the previous day, and the food wrapped and refrigerated, so when you return all that has to be done is remove the meal from the refrigerator, unwrap it and then sit, enjoy the meal and relax.

Savoury and sweet ideas are included in this section. Main meals such as Eastern Chicken (page 62) and desserts, for instance Tropical Mousse (page 70), are suitable for everyday family meals as well as more elaborate dinner parties or buffets. Buffet meals can cause endless problems as their success depends on advance preparation. By serving a wide selection of cold dishes it is possible to lay the table and display the food before guests arrive, then all that has to be done is remove empty dishes and replace them with fresh ones when necessary. This eliminates constant dashes from oven to table as well as worry about the meal. Any excess food can be wrapped, refrigerated and, when suitable, served the next day. Another section is devoted to recipes for entertaining, so make use of all the suggestions.

When people think of cold food they conjure up a picture of unappetising meals consisting of wilting lettuce leaves, wedges of tomato and limp cucumber. Lentil Rice Salad (page 56) and Bean Bonanza (page 53) are two of the more imaginative dishes. By all means accompany them with crisp green or mixed salads, but try these as well!

COLD CONCOCTIONS

All recipes marked * are suitable for vegetarians as well as non-vegetarians

CREAMY LEEK FLAN

SERVES 6

225 CALORIES PER SERVING

If this flan is made some hours before serving the light green colour will turn a little grey, but this doesn't alter the flavour.

8 oatcakes

8 teaspoons margarine

1lb (480g) leeks, sliced

6oz (180g) curd cheese

1 teaspoon lemon juice

salt and pepper

2½ teaspoons aspic powder

1 egg white

pinch of cream of tartar

6 cherry tomatoes, sliced

Tip:
Egg whites from eggs stored at room temperature whisk to a greater volume than those kept in a refrigerator, therefore remove eggs from the refrigerator about an hour before use.

1. Crush the oatcakes to form crumbs. Melt the margarine and stir in the oatcake crumbs. Press the mixture onto the base of a 7-inch (17.5-cm) springform tin.
2. Boil the leeks in a little water for about 15 minutes until soft. Drain, reserve the cooking liquid and transfer the leeks to a food processor or blender.
3. Add the curd cheese and lemon juice to the leeks and process until smooth. Spoon the leek purée into a bowl and season well with salt and pepper.
4. Measure 2 tablespoons of the reserved cooking liquid into a cup or small basin, sprinkle in the aspic powder and stand in a saucepan of simmering water until dissolved.
5. Stir the dissolved aspic into the leek purée and leave until beginning to set.
6. Whisk the egg white with the cream of tartar until peaking, then fold into the setting leek purée. Spoon over the oatcake base and chill until set.
7. Open the side of the springform tin and transfer the Creamy Leek Flan to a serving plate. Garnish with slices of cherry tomatoes and serve.

Selections per serving:
   1 Bread
   1 Fat
   ½ Protein
   1 Vegetable
   45 Optional Calories

CUCUMBER CHIMNEYS

SERVES 4

35 CALORIES PER SERVING

Choose a wide cucumber for this recipe so there is plenty of room for the filling. If only thin cucumbers are available use 2 × 1-inch (2.5-cm) pieces.

4 × 1½-inch (4-cm) thick slices of cucumber, peeled

salt

2oz (60g) white crabmeat – fresh, frozen or canned with as much liquid as possible drained off

1oz (30g) fromage frais

8 capers, finely chopped

½ teaspoon tomato purée

2 teaspoons low-calorie mayonnaise

few drops of pepper sauce

few leaves of radicchio, shredded

4 sprigs of parsley

> **Tip:**
> The Cucumber Chimneys may be arranged on one large plate and served at a buffet meal.

1. Remove the seeds from each piece of cucumber using an apple corer or a knife and teaspoon. Sprinkle well with salt and leave for 20 minutes, then drain and rinse under running cold water. It is important to remove all traces of salt or the flavour will spoil the recipe. Pat the cucumber dry with paper towels.
2. Mix the crabmeat together with the fromage frais, capers, tomato purée and mayonnaise. Season the mixture to taste with the pepper sauce (don't add any salt).
3. Spoon the crabmeat mixture into the centre of each piece of cucumber.
4. Arrange the shredded radicchio leaves on four small plates. Place each Cucumber Chimney in the centre and garnish with a sprig of parsley.

Selections per serving:
- ¼ Fat
- ½ Protein
- ½ Vegetable
- 10 Optional Calories

TIT BITS

The following recipes are ideal cocktail snacks but, alternatively, arrange them on a bed of lettuce and serve as hors d'œuvres.

CREAMY TOMATOES (Serves 6) 85 Calories per Serving

15 cherry tomatoes – approximately 4oz (120g)

3 black olives, pitted and chopped

2 teaspoons finely chopped chives

4½ tablespoons cream cheese

1 tablespoon single cream

dash of pepper sauce

Selections per serving:
   85 Optional Calories

1. Cut the tomatoes in half and scoop out all the seeds with a coffee spoon or the end of a teaspoon. Sprinkle the chopped olives and chives into the halves.
2. Mix the cream cheese together with the cream then season with the pepper sauce. Chill until the mixture is stiff, about an hour.
3. Spoon a little of the cheese mixture on each tomato half, or alternatively use a ⅜-inch (1-cm) nozzle to pipe the mixture on top – this is more difficult but looks very attractive.

CELERY BOATS (Serves 6) 40 Calories per Serving

3 sticks celery

1½oz (45g) Danish blue cheese

3oz (90g) fromage frais

2oz (60g) well-drained canned mandarin segments

Selections per serving:
   ½ Protein
   ¼ Vegetable
   5 Optional Calories

1. Cut the celery into 1½-inch (4-cm) lengths. If necessary cut a thin slice from the rounded side of the celery so it lays flat.
2. Mash the cheese with a little fromage frais until smooth then mix in the remaining fromage frais.
3. Spoon or pipe the cheese mixture using a ⅜-inch (1-cm) nozzle inside each piece of celery.
4. Cut each mandarin segment into three or four pieces and place one piece on each celery boat.

GRAPE SANDWICHES Vegetarian (Serves 6) 45 Calories per serving

24 large black grapes, 7–8oz (210–240g)

2oz (60g) curd cheese

½oz (15g) walnuts, finely chopped

1½ teaspoons low-fat natural yogurt

1. Cut each grape in half and scoop out the pips using the tip of a sharp knife.
2. Mix the curd cheese, walnuts and yogurt together and sandwich the halves of each grape with the nutty mixture.

Selections per serving:
   45 Optional Calories

Tip:
These can be made in advance and refrigerated.

MUSHROOM AND CHICK PEA PÂTÉ

SERVES 6

65 CALORIES PER SERVING

If you cut down the preparation of this recipe by using canned chick peas, don't use the liquid from the can as it would make the pâté too salty.

9oz (270g) freshly cooked or drained canned chick peas, reserve ¼ pint (150ml) of the cooking liquid

3oz (90g) onion

5½oz (165g) flat mushrooms

2 teaspoons margarine

1 sachet aspic powder

1 teaspoon mushroom ketchup

2 stuffed olives

1–2 small button mushrooms (optional)

Tip:
Serve with salad or melba toast.

1. Place the cooked chick peas and ¼ pint (150ml) of the cooking liquid into a blender or food processor – if using canned chick peas drain well and add ¼ pint (150ml) water.
2. Chop the onion and 4oz (120g) mushrooms.
3. Heat the margarine in a saucepan, add the onion and stir-fry for 5 minutes or until translucent. Stir the chopped mushrooms into the saucepan and stir-fry for 1 minute then cover the saucepan, reduce the heat and leave for 5 minutes.
4. Pour 4 tablespoons hot water into a cup or small basin, sprinkle in the aspic and place in a saucepan of simmering water until dissolved.
5. Add the mushroom ketchup and cooked onion and mushrooms to the chick peas. Transfer to a food processor or blender and process the mixture until smooth. Reserve 1 teaspoon of the dissolved aspic. Pour the remainder into the purée and process once again. Finely chop the remaining flat mushrooms and fold into the purée.
6. Spoon the mixture into a serving dish.
7. Place the cup or basin with the remaining aspic in a saucepan of simmering water and leave until dissolved. Stir in 3 tablespoons water.
8. Rinse the olives and slice as thinly as possible (each olive should cut into 8 or 9 slices). If using button mushrooms slice as thinly as possible. Arrange the olive and mushroom slices on top of the pâté and cover with a very thin layer of the aspic. Chill once again until set.

Selections per serving:
½ Protein
¼ Vegetable
15 Optional Calories

BEAN BONANZA

SERVES 4

205 CALORIES PER SERVING

When broad beans are slipped out of their waxy skins their colour changes from dull grey to an attractive bright green.

3oz (90g) shelled broad beans or frozen broad beans

2 tomatoes

6oz (180g) mixture of freshly cooked or drained canned red and white kidney beans

¼ medium avocado, approximately 2oz (60g)

3oz (90g) Cambazola or blue brie, diced

2–3 teaspoons chopped chives

1½oz (45g) rashers lean smoked back bacon, rind removed

2 tablespoons lemon juice

1 tablespoon olive oil

¼ teaspoon Dijon mustard

salt and pepper

Tip:
Store the remaining avocado, with the stone in place, in the refrigerator; this slows down browning.

1. Plunge the fresh beans into boiling water, return to the boil and cook for about 12 minutes (cook frozen beans for about 4 minutes). Drain, cool and slide them out of their waxy skins into a bowl.
2. Cover the tomatoes with boiling water, leave for 30 seconds, drain and slip their skins off. Cut in half, scoop out and discard the seeds and chop the flesh.
3. Mix the broad beans together with the tomatoes and kidney beans.
4. Roughly chop the avocado and stir into the beans with the cheese and chives.
5. Place the bacon on the rack of a grill pan and grill, turning once, until crisp. Allow to cool then chop or crumble the bacon into the bean mixture.
6. Place the lemon juice, oil, mustard and a little salt and pepper into a screw-top jar, secure and shake well. Alternatively whisk them together in a small basin. Pour the dressing over the salad and toss.

Selections per serving:
1 Fat
2 Protein
¾ Vegetable
10 Optional Calories

ORANGE-DRESSED SALAD

SERVES 4

70 CALORIES PER SERVING

The mint and orange dressing adds a tang to the vegetables.

½ yellow pepper

2 carrots

3 sticks celery

I small courgette

2–3 spring onions

I small or ½ medium apple

4 tablespoons orange juice

2 teaspoons finely chopped mint

4 teaspoons olive oil

few lettuce, chicory or endive leaves

Tip:
If you wish to make this salad an hour or more before serving, toss the apple in a little lemon juice before adding to the other ingredients. This will delay the browning of the fruit.

1. Remove and discard the seeds from the pepper. Cut the pepper, carrots, celery and courgette into thin I-inch (2.5-cm) lengths.
2. Cut the spring onions in half lengthways then cut into I-inch (2.5-cm) lengths.
3. Quarter and core the apple, then cut into pieces roughly the same size as the vegetables.
4. Whisk the orange juice, mint and oil together. Pour the dressing over the salad ingredients and toss well.
5. Arrange the salad leaves round the edge of the serving dish or bowl then pile the salad in the centre.

Selections per serving:
I Fat
¼ Fruit
I Vegetable

LENTIL RICE SALAD

SERVES 6

155 CALORIES PER SERVING

Any variety of long-grain rice can be used for this recipe but the combination of lentils and basmati rice is especially good.

6oz (180g) green lentils

½ onion, chopped

¾ pint (450ml) water

4oz (120g) frozen petit pois

3oz (90g) long-grain rice

2 tomatoes

3 tablespoons low-fat natural yogurt

1–2 teaspoons Madras curry powder

1 teaspoon wine vinegar

Tip:
Decorate the salad with coriander leaves; this looks pretty and the flavour blends well with the curry spices.

1. Rinse the lentils then place in a saucepan with the onion and water. Bring to the boil, cover and boil for 10 minutes, then reduce the heat and simmer for 15 minutes. Add the petit pois and cook for a further 4–5 minutes. Drain off any excess water.

2. Boil the rice according to the packaging instructions. If necessary drain off any excess water to leave the grains fluffy and separate.

3. Cover the tomatoes with boiling water, leave for 30 seconds then slip off their skins. Cut each tomato in half, scoop out and discard the seeds and roughly chop the flesh.

4. Mix the warm lentils together with the peas and rice. Stir in the chopped tomatoes.

5. Stir the yogurt, curry powder and vinegar together. Stir the dressing through the lentil mixture. Leave until completely cold then cover and refrigerate until the salad is to be served.

Selections per serving:
 ½ Bread
 1 Protein
 ½ Vegetable
 5 Optional Calories

PEPPERED BULGAR

SERVES 4

135 CALORIES PER SERVING

Bulgar wheat is now sold in many supermarkets as well as healthfood shops and delicatessens.

4oz (120g) bulgar wheat

½ pint (300ml) boiling water

1 medium red pepper

1 medium yellow pepper

1 medium green pepper

½ red onion, finely chopped

3 tablespoons low-calorie French dressing

1–2 teaspoons paprika

Tip:
Make this salad a few hours before it is to be served so the peppery flavour has sufficient time to penetrate through the bulgar.

1. Place the bulgar in a bowl, pour over the boiling water and leave for 30 minutes. Transfer to a clean cloth and squeeze out any water so the bulgar is dry and separate.
2. Lay the three peppers on the rack of a grill pan and grill for about 10 minutes, turning three or four times so the pepper skins are completely charred. Plunge the peppers into a bowl of cold water.
3. When the peppers are cool enough to handle pull off the charred skins, cut in half and remove and discard the seeds. Finely chop the peppers and place in a bowl with the chopped onion. Stir in the bulgar wheat.
4. Mix the French dressing and paprika together then pour over the pepper mixture and toss well to coat all the ingredients. Cover and refrigerate until ready to serve.

Selections per serving:
1 Bread
½ Fat
1 Vegetable
5 Optional Calories

RADISH AND ORANGE SALAD

SERVES 4

30 CALORIES PER SERVING

If possible buy seedless oranges for this salad, they are much easier to slice thinly. The sharp flavour of the oranges make this salad a good accompaniment to oily fish such as mackerel.

2 medium oranges

12–14 radishes

2 tablespoons low-calorie salad dressing

3–4 teaspoons chopped chives

½ teaspoon lemon juice

Tip:
When serving this salad at a special meal surround it with pretty green salad leaves.

1. Using a sharp knife remove the skin and white pith from the oranges and cut in very thin slices. Cut the large slices in quarters, the smaller ones in half.
2. Thinly slice the radishes, mix with the prepared oranges and arrange in a serving dish.
3. Mix the salad dressing, chives and lemon juice together and spoon over the salad.

Selections per serving:
   ¼ Fat
   ½ Fruit
   ¼ Vegetable
   5 Optional Calories

CEVICHE

SERVES 4

120 CALORIES PER SERVING

This is a Mexican recipe. The fish is 'cooked' by marinating in an extremely acid liquid which covers the fish completely. This causes a chemical reaction which changes the nature of the fish.

1lb (480g) cod or haddock fillet

4 limes

4 lemons

1 clove garlic, crushed

1 teaspoon mild chilli powder

salt

1 small onion, sliced

2 red peppers

2 tablespoons finely chopped coriander

Tip:
Use only fresh fish for this recipe – it is not advisable to use frozen.

1. Remove the skin from the fish and cut into strips no larger than 2 × ½-inch (5 × 1.25-cm).
2. Squeeze the juice from the limes and lemons and add the garlic, chilli powder and salt.
3. Place the fish and onion in a non-metallic dish and pour the marinade over to cover the fish completely – if necessary add more lemon or lime juice. Cover the dish with clingfilm and refrigerate for 12–24 hours.
4. Lay the peppers on the rack of a grill pan and cook under a moderate heat, turning three or four times, until completely charred. Transfer to a bowl of cold water until cool enough to handle then peel off the skins, remove the seeds and cut into thin strips.
5. Drain the fish and onion, stir in the strips of red pepper and coriander and serve.

Selections per serving:
  3 Protein
  ½ Vegetable

JULIENNE MEAT MIX

SERVES 4

235 CALORIES PER SERVING

Serve this recipe with a mixed salad and baked potato or warm crusty bread to make a complete meal.

5oz (150g) cooked ox tongue

5oz (150g) cooked beef

6 medium kumquats

4oz (120g) parsnips

salt

2 tablespoons olive oil

4 teaspoons wine vinegar

½ teaspoon Dijon mustard

salt and pepper

salad leaves

2–3 teaspoons chopped chives

Tip:
As ox tongue is fairly expensive substitute cooked ham for some or all of it.

1. Cut the cooked meats into ¼ × ¼ × 1½-inch (5-mm × 5-mm × 4-cm) lengths and place in a bowl.
2. Cut the kumquats in half lengthways, cut each half lengthways into three pieces and add to the meat.
3. Cut the parsnips in sticks the same size as the meat and boil in salted water for about 8 minutes until cooked, drain and add to the meat.
4. Whisk the oil together with the vinegar and mustard, alternatively place in a screw-top jar and shake well to mix. Season with salt and pepper and mix again.
5. Pour the dressing over the meat mixture and toss well.
6. Arrange the salad leaves in a salad bowl, toss the salad once again and spoon on top of the leaves. Sprinkle the chives over the meat.

Selections per serving:
  1½ Fat
  ½ Fruit
  2½ Protein
  ¼ Vegetable

 VEGETARIAN

GREEN SALAD

SERVES 2

530 CALORIES PER SERVING

Serve this with a tomato and onion salad to make a complete meal.

3oz (90g) small pasta shapes

salt

4 spring onions

1oz (30g) pistachio nuts

6oz (180g) freshly cooked or drained canned flageolet beans

1 small courgette, diced

2 teaspoons pumpkin seeds

3oz (90g) mixture green beans and broccoli florets

2 teaspoons olive oil

1 tablespoon lime or lemon juice

1 clove garlic, crushed

2 tablespoons finely chopped basil

salt and pepper

2oz (60g) sage Derby cheese

few green salad leaves

> **Tip:**
> If fresh green beans and broccoli are not available substitute with frozen beans, broccoli or peas and boil for three minutes.

1. Boil the pasta in salted water according to the packaging instructions.
2. While the pasta is cooking thickly slice the spring onions and roughly chop the pistachio nuts.
3. Mix the spring onions together with the pistachio nuts, flageolet beans and courgette. Stir in the pumpkin seeds.
4. Cut the green beans into 1-inch (2.5-cm) lengths, plunge into boiling water and cook for 5 minutes. Cut the broccoli into tiny florets then add to the beans and boil for a further 3 minutes.
5. Drain the hot pasta and mix together with the pistachio nut mixture, beans and broccoli.
6. Place the oil, lime or lemon juice, garlic, chopped basil and a little salt and pepper in a small jar, secure and shake well, or alternatively whisk in a small basin. Pour the dressing over the pasta salad, toss well and leave until cool.
7. Cut the cheese into small cubes and mix into the salad. Arrange the salad leaves on a serving plate and pile the salad in the centre.

Selections per serving:
  1½ Bread
  1½ Fat
  3 Protein
  1¼ Vegetable
  20 Optional Calories

EASTERN CHICKEN

SERVES 4

320 CALORIES PER SERVING

This salad keeps well so it can be made in advance, covered and refrigerated. Toss the salad before serving.

1oz (30g) pitted prunes

1oz (30g) dried apricots

4 tablespoons orange juice

6oz (180g) bulgar wheat

12fl oz (360ml) boiling chicken stock

2oz (60g) baby corn on the cob

salt

2 small courgettes

10oz (300g) cooked chicken

½-inch (1.25-cm) slice fresh ginger

3 tablespoons low-calorie French dressing

few lettuce, radicchio or endive leaves

Tip:
To make a complete meal serve with a green or mixed salad.

1. Roughly chop the prunes and apricots, cover with the orange juice and leave for several hours or overnight.
2. Place the bulgar wheat in a bowl. Pour the boiling stock over the bulgar wheat and leave for 30 minutes. Transfer to a clean cloth and squeeze as hard as possible to remove excess stock.
3. Thickly slice the baby corn on the cob, boil in salted water for about 10 minutes until cooked, drain.
4. Chop the courgettes, mix together with the bulgar wheat and corn. Drain the soaked fruits, reserve any remaining orange juice and stir into the bulgar wheat mixture.
5. Roughly chop or slice the chicken and stir into the salad ingredients.
6. Roughly chop the ginger and press it through a garlic press to extract its juice. Mix the ginger juice and low-calorie dressing with any remaining orange juice. Stir the dressing through the salad.
7. Arrange the salad leaves round the edge of a bowl and pile the salad in the centre.

Selections per serving:
1½ Bread
½ Fat
½ Fruit
2½ Protein
½ Vegetable
20 Optional Calories

Eastern Chicken

CRISPY-TOPPED FRUIT

SERVES 4

200 CALORIES PER SERVING

The 8% fat fromage frais gives a creamy flavour to this recipe but, if you prefer, substitute with the lower fat variety.

1 tablespoon margarine

1 teaspoon honey

3oz (90g) muesli

1lb (480g) drained canned apricots, plums or peaches

8oz (240g) fromage frais

Tip:
The topping can be made in advance then, when completely cold, stored in an airtight container.

1. Gently heat the margarine and honey in a small saucepan until dissolved.
2. Place the muesli in a bowl, pour over the margarine and honey and mix well to coat all the muesli.
3. Cover a baking sheet with a layer of aluminium foil. Spread the muesli thinly and evenly over the foil. Place under a moderate grill until golden. Leave to cool.
4. Arrange the fruit in four serving glasses. Spoon the fromage frais over the fruit then sprinkle the cold crisp muesli over the top. Serve immediately or the muesli will lose its crisp texture.

Selections per serving:
¾ Bread
¾ Fat
1 Fruit
1 Protein
5 Optional Calories

MOCHA APRICOT DESSERT

SERVES 3

90 CALORIES PER SERVING

Coffee granules vary in strength so add sufficient to suit your taste.

1 tablespoon cornflour

7½fl oz (225ml) skimmed milk

1 egg, beaten

1 teaspoon demerara sugar

1–1½ teaspoons instant coffee granules

6 medium apricots

Tip:
If you drink sweet coffee you may want to add a little artificial sweetener.

1. Blend the cornflour to a smooth paste with a little milk. Reserve 3–4 tablespoons milk and stir the remainder into the cornflour.
2. Heat the cornflour and milk until boiling, stirring all the time. Simmer for 1–2 minutes, stirring continuously, then remove from the heat and allow to cool a little.
3. Stir the reserved milk into the beaten egg then strain into the cool sauce. Return to a very low heat and stir all the time until the sauce begins to thicken. Do not boil.
4. Remove the hot sauce from the heat and stir in the sugar and coffee granules.
5. Remove the stones from the apricots, roughly chop and divide between three serving glasses. Pour the coffee sauce over the apricots and leave until cold. Chill until ready to serve.

Selections per serving:
1 Fruit
¼ Milk
45 Optional Calories

CHOCOLATE CUPS

SERVES 6

220 CALORIES PER SERVING

This recipe requires care and patience as making the chocolate cases takes some time. Use any type of chocolate – plain, milk, white or half of one and the rest of another.

5oz (150g) chocolate

6 medium apricots or 3 medium peaches, stoned

4½oz (135g) chestnut purée

2 tablespoons skimmed milk

2 tablespoons caster sugar

Tip:
Place the Chocolate Cups in the freezer for a few minutes before removing the paper cases.

1. Break the chocolate into small pieces, place in a bowl and stand in a saucepan of simmering water until melted.
2. Arrange six double thicknesses of paper cases in pastry cutters or patty tins to prevent them spreading out.
3. Brush the melted chocolate evenly over the inside of each of the six cases. Chill each case as it is completed, then brush the others with the remaining chocolate. Return the bowl of chocolate to the saucepan of hot water when necessary and give each case a second coat until the chocolate is used up.
4. Chop 4 apricots or 2 peaches; cut the remainder into wedges. Blend the chestnut purée, milk and sugar together and spoon into a piping bag fitted with a ¾-inch (2-cm) fluted nozzle.
5. Place the chocolate cases flat on a plate, very gently pull the paper cases back, then lift off the base.
6. Divide the fruit between each chocolate case and pipe a swirl of chestnut purée on top. Decorate with reserved wedges of fruit.

Selections per serving:
¼ Bread
½ Fruit
145 Optional Calories

FRUITY CHOCOLATE MOUSSE

SERVES 4

155 CALORIES PER SERVING

Serve this mousse in one dish or four tall glasses or large ramekins of about 8fl oz (240ml) capacity.

3 tablespoons cocoa

½ pint (300ml) skimmed milk

artificial sweetener

¼ teaspoon vanilla essence

3 tablespoons black coffee

2½ teaspoons gelatine

12oz (360g) well-drained canned sliced peaches, apricots or mandarins

1 large egg white

pinch of cream of tartar

4½ tablespoons double cream

Tip:
To make this recipe suitable for a vegetarian substitute gelatine with a vegetable-based gelling agent.

---

1. Mix the cocoa to a smooth paste with a little milk. Heat the remaining milk until steaming then gradually stir into the cocoa.
2. Sweeten the cocoa with artificial sweetener equivalent to 4–5 tablespoons of sugar, then stir in the vanilla essence.
3. Measure the black coffee into a cup or small basin and sprinkle in the gelatine. Stand the cup in a saucepan of simmering water and leave until the gelatine has completely dissolved.
4. Stir the dissolved gelatine into the cocoa and milk, then place in the refrigerator until almost set – stir occasionally to prevent a skin forming.
5. Chop the fruit and divide equally between four large ramekins or glasses.
6. Whisk the egg white and cream of tartar until peaking. Whisk the cocoa mixture until the consistency of an egg white. Fold the whisked egg into the cocoa and spoon on top of the chopped fruit. Refrigerate until set.
7. Whisk the cream until it holds its shape then spoon or pipe on top of the chocolate mousse.

Selections per serving:
¾ Fruit
¼ Milk
80 Optional Calories

PINEAPPLE AND CHOCOLATE

SERVES 4

210 CALORIES PER SERVING

This dessert combines three different flavours and textures – firm, juicy pineapple with a smooth, creamy orange mix, topped with crunchy chocolate.

1½oz (45g) chocolate

4 teaspoons low-fat spread

1oz (30g) cornflakes

1lb (480g) pineapple

3oz (90g) fromage frais

3oz (90g) curd cheese

3 tablespoons frozen concentrated orange juice

3 tablespoons low-fat natural yogurt

Tip:
To prevent the chocolate breaking into small pieces when cutting into triangles, use a slightly warm, very sharp knife.

1. Melt the chocolate and low-fat spread in a bowl resting on a saucepan of simmering water. Lightly crush the cornflakes then stir into the melted chocolate.
2. Using the back of a spoon spread the chocolate mixture on a sheet of non-stick baking parchment to form a thin square. Chill until set.
3. Dice the pineapple and divide between four serving glasses.
4. Mix the fromage frais together with the curd cheese, concentrated orange juice and yogurt.
5. Cut the chocolate square into four smaller squares, then cut each square diagonally in two to make a total of eight triangles.
6. Just before serving spoon the cheese and orange mixture on top of the pineapple and decorate each dessert with two chocolate triangles.

Selections per serving:
¼ Bread
½ Fat
1¼ Fruit
¾ Protein
70 Optional Calories

TROPICAL MOUSSE

SERVES 6

65 CALORIES PER SERVING

This blend of exotic fruits makes a wonderful dessert, ideal for a simple lunch or an extra special dinner party.

1½ medium mangoes

4oz (120g) crushed pineapple

½ medium banana

finely grated zest of ½ a medium orange

juice of 1 medium orange

1 tablespoon gelatine

2 egg whites

pinch of cream of tartar

2 teaspoons caster sugar

1 fig or kiwi fruit, sliced

Tip:
To make this recipe suitable for a vegetarian substitute gelatine with a vegetable-based gelling agent.

1. Scrape all the flesh attached to the mango skins and stones into a blender or food processor. Add the crushed pineapple, banana and orange zest and process until smooth. Pour into a bowl.
2. Pour the orange juice into a small basin or cup. Sprinkle the gelatine into the juice and stir. Stand the basin in a saucepan of simmering water and leave until dissolved.
3. Stir the dissolved gelatine into the fruit purée and leave until beginning to set.
4. Whisk the egg whites and cream of tartar until peaking. Add the sugar and whisk again.
5. Fold the egg whites into the setting purée and spoon into six ramekins or glasses. Chill until set then decorate with the fig or kiwi fruit.

Selections per serving:
    1 Fruit
    20 Optional Calories

STRIPY SUNDAE

SERVES 3

195 CALORIES PER SERVING

Choose a ripe avocado for this recipe. To judge how ripe the fruit is squeeze gently – the skin should 'give' a little.

5oz (150g) raspberries

1 teaspoon clear honey

10oz (300g) fromage frais

½ medium avocado, approximately 4oz (120g)

1 medium banana

2 teaspoons lemon juice

Tip:
Avocados vary considerably in size; 4oz (120g) can be all the flesh of one yet only half of another, so always weigh them stoned and peeled.

1. Reserve a few raspberries for decoration. Place the remainder in the goblet of a blender. Add the honey and 4oz (120g) fromage frais, then process until smooth.
2. Mash the avocado, banana and lemon juice until smooth. Gradually mix in the remaining fromage frais.
3. Place a tablespoonful of the avocado mixture into each of three small stemmed wine glasses. Spoon the raspberry purée on top of the avocado, then cover with the remaining avocado purée.
4. Decorate with the reserved raspberries.

Selections per serving:
1 Fat
1 Fruit
1½ Protein
20 Optional Calories

FAST
FOOD

With today's hectic way of life people seem to be hurrying from one thing to another and it is all too easy to skip meals, become hungry and then eat several snacks or quickly buy a take-away. However it is possible to make tasty, nutritious meals in a very short time and this will help prevent nibbling to satisfy hunger. This section is comprised of recipes which can be made in 30 minutes or less. There are dishes for one, two or more people, and the ideas include snacks, main meals and desserts.

The most important factor to be considered when preparing food within a limited time is organisation. While the food which requires the longest cooking time is cooking, prepare the remaining ingredients. For example, while pasta is boiling, make a salad to accompany it and turn it into a balanced meal. The order of work in these recipes has been written and tested to keep preparation time as short as possible, so follow the method carefully.

Make maximum use of processed or partially prepared foods such as frozen peas, canned beans etc. which are kept in the kitchen storecupboard. They can be included in the recipe or served alongside it. If time allows, make a list and do the shopping in advance. Consider which methods are suitable for cooking quickly; kebabs can be prepared in minutes, stir-frys take very little time to cook and salads are easily put together.

Perhaps the most important thing to remember when preparing food for yourself, and even more so when entertaining and you have very little time, is don't panic!

FAST FOOD

All recipes marked * are suitable for vegetarians as well as non-vegetarians

SPINACH NOODLES

SERVES 2

420 CALORIES PER SERVING

This tasty recipe can be rustled up in no time at all.

4oz (120g) noodles, e.g. tagliatelle

salt

8oz (240g) frozen leaf spinach

2–3 spring onions, roughly chopped

2 tablespoons cream cheese

2 eggs

½oz (15g) Parmesan cheese, finely grated

Tip:
1lb (480g) fresh spinach may be used in place of the frozen variety. Wash the leaves, shake to remove excess water then place in a saucepan, cover and cook for 5–6 minutes until limp.

1. Cook the noodles in boiling salted water according to the packaging instructions.
2. Cook the spinach according to the packaging instructions then drain well to remove all of the excess water.
3. Place the drained spinach, spring onions, cream cheese and eggs in a blender or food processor and process until the ingredients form a smooth purée.
4. Drain the noodles then return to the saucepan and pour in the spinach purée. Cook over a low heat, stirring all the time, until the eggs are just cooked and the purée is thick.
5. Spoon the Spinach Noodles onto two warm serving plates and sprinkle with Parmesan cheese.

Selections per serving:
  2 Bread
  1¼ Protein
  1½ Vegetable
  100 Optional Calories

 VEGETARIAN

CRISPY CAULIFLOWER

SERVES 4

225 CALORIES PER SERVING

This recipe is quick to make and is an ideal lunch or supper dish.

4oz (120g) green beans

8oz (240g) small cauliflower florets

salt

2 teaspoons margarine

½oz (15g) flour

4 tablespoons skimmed milk

4oz (120g) fromage frais

4oz (120g) brie, outer rind removed (weight after rind removed)

1oz (30g) blanched almonds

1½oz (45g) fresh breadcumbs

Tip:
Save money by blanching your own almonds. Cover them with boiling water, leave for 2 minutes, drain, and then slip off their skins.

1. Cut the beans into 1½-inch (4-cm) lengths.
2. Cook the cauliflower in boiling salted water for 2–3 minutes, then add the beans and cook for a further 6 minutes until cooked but still crisp. Drain well.
3. Heat the margarine in a saucepan, add the flour, stir well, then remove from the heat.
4. Gradually blend the milk, then the fromage frais into the flour. Return to the heat then bring to the boil, stirring all the time.
5. Cut the brie into very small pieces. Add to the sauce and stir over a very low heat until the brie has melted. Stir in the drained vegetables then transfer to the serving dish.
6. Roughly chop the almonds, mix with the breadcrumbs and scatter over the vegetables. Place under a hot grill until brown.

Selections per serving:
   ½ Bread
   ¾ Fat
   2 Protein
   1 Vegetable
   5 Optional Calories

AVOCADO, GRAPEFRUIT AND CHEESE

SERVES 4

140 CALORIES PER SERVING

This refreshing salad makes an ideal starter for four people but could be accompanied by wholemeal crusty bread to make a snack meal for two.

1 medium grapefruit

3oz (90g) avocado

8 large black olives, pitted

4oz (120g) mozzarella or feta cheese

a few radicchio or lettuce leaves

Tip:
Don't remove the stone from the part of avocado not required for this recipe – it will help to slow down discolouration.

1. Peel the grapefruit, divide into segments and carefully remove all the membranes to leave whole segments.
2. Thinly slice the avocado along its length.
3. Cut the black olives into quarters.
4. Chop the cheese into small pieces.
5. Mix the grapefruit, avocado, black olives and cheese gently together.
6. Lay a few radicchio or lettuce leaves on each serving plate, spoon a quarter of the salad on each and serve immediately before the avocado discolours.

Selections per serving:
   1 Fat
   ½ Fruit
   1 Protein
   5 Optional Calories

Avocado, Grapefruit and Cheese

CHICKEN RISOTTO

SERVES 2

475 CALORIES PER SERVING

Use either chicken breasts or thighs. Boneless thighs are now sold in many supermarkets.

4oz (120g) long-grain rice

I tablespoon oil

I small clove garlic, chopped

I½ teaspoons hot Madras curry powder

8oz (240g) boneless skinned chicken cut in 1-inch (2.5-cm) cubes

½ large red or yellow pepper, seeded and chopped

1oz (30g) water chestnuts, chopped

4 spring onions cut in 1-inch (2.5-cm) lengths

½oz (15g) raisins

½ medium banana, roughly chopped

5 tablespoons low-fat natural yogurt

squeeze of lemon juice

salt

I½ teaspoons garam masala

Tip:
Leave the remaining banana half in its skin, brush the cut face with lemon juice for use the next day.

1. Cook the rice according to the packaging instructions and keep warm. The grains must be fluffy and separate.
2. Heat the oil in a saucepan, add the garlic and stir-fry for I minute. Add the curry powder, then the chicken, and stir-fry for about 10 minutes until the chicken is cooked.
3. Add the pepper, water chestnuts and spring onions to the saucepan and stir-fry for 2 minutes.
4. Add the hot rice, raisins, banana and yogurt to the saucepan and stir over a moderate heat for 2 minutes.
5. Season the chicken and rice with a little lemon juice and salt. Remove from the heat, stir in the garam masala and spoon onto two warm serving plates.

Selections per serving:
   2 Bread
   1½ Fat
   ¾ Fruit
   ¼ Milk
   3 Protein
   ½ Vegetable
   10 Optional Calories

CHICKEN BALLS IN CREAM SAUCE

SERVES 4

180 CALORIES PER SERVING

Use a thick-bottomed saucepan to prevent the milk burning.

12oz (360g) boneless skinned chicken

1oz (30g) fresh breadcrumbs

¼ teaspoon tarragon

finely grated zest of ¼ of a lemon

1 egg white

8fl oz (240ml) skimmed milk

1 onion ring

1 tablespoon cornflour

4 tablespoons single cream

chopped parsley

Tip:
Serve with brightly coloured vegetables such as green beans and carrots.

1. Roughly chop the chicken then place in a food processor with the breadcrumbs, tarragon and lemon zest. Process for a few seconds then add the egg white and process again to mix. Alternatively finely mince the chicken, stir in the breadcrumbs, tarragon and lemon zest and mix well. Lightly beat the egg white and mix into the chicken mixture.
2. Using dampened hands shape the chicken mixture into sixteen balls.
3. Pour the milk into a medium-sized saucepan large enough to hold all the chicken balls in one layer. Add the onion ring and heat until steaming. Add the chicken balls, cover and simmer gently for 15 minutes.
4. Remove the chicken balls with a slotted spoon and keep warm while completing the sauce.
5. Blend the cornflour to a smooth paste with the cream. Stir into the hot milk and bring to the boil, stirring all the time. Pour the cream sauce over the chicken and sprinkle with chopped parsley.

Selections per serving:
¼ Bread
2½ Protein
65 Optional Calories

STEAK AU POIVRE

SERVES 2

305 CALORIES PER SERVING

A dinner party in less than 30 minutes!

1½–2 teaspoons black peppercorns

2 × 5oz (150g) fillet steaks

¼ onion

2½ teaspoons margarine

1oz (30g) mushrooms, finely chopped

1 tablespoon brandy

3 tablespoons single cream

salt

Tip:
Serve with a mixed salad which can be prepared between steps 2 and 3.

1. Crush the peppercorns using a pestle and mortar or place in a bowl and crush with the end of a rolling pin. Sprinkle evenly over a plate.
2. Turn the steaks in the peppercorns, pressing them firmly onto the meat, then put to one side.
3. Finely chop the onion (there should be about 2 tablespoons). Preheat the grill.
4. Melt 2 teaspoons margarine in a small frying pan, add the onion and stir round. Leave over a low heat for about 6 minutes, stirring occasionally.
5. Lay the steaks on the rack of a grill pan and place about 2½ inches (7.5cm) away from a hot grill. Cook for 6–7 minutes, turning once, until the fat stops dripping (there should hardly be any fat from lean fillet steak).
6. Increase the heat to moderate under the frying pan, add the steaks and cook for 40–50 seconds each side for medium rare – a little longer if you prefer a well done steak.
7. Transfer the steaks to a plate and keep warm. Add the remaining margarine to the frying pan, stir in the mushrooms and cook for 2 minutes.
8. Spoon any juices which have run from the steaks into the frying pan, add the brandy, then the cream, and allow to bubble for 1 minute. Season with a little salt and spoon half beside each steak.

Selections per serving:
1¼ Fat
4 Protein
¼ Vegetable
65 Optional Calories

PORK WITH LYCHEES

SERVES 4

250 CALORIES PER SERVING

This recipe proves that a tasty meal can be prepared in a short while if an organised method is followed.

14oz (420g) pork tenderloin

16 lychees

4oz (120g) mange-tout

2 teaspoons cornflour

1 tablespoon lemon juice

juice of ½ a medium orange

1 tablespoon soy sauce

½ teaspoon sugar

4 teaspoons oil

12oz (360g) beansprouts

Tip:
Use the remaining orange in a fresh fruit salad.

1. Lay the pork on the rack of a grill pan and grill, turning once, until the fat stops dripping from the meat. Allow to cool.
2. While grilling the pork, skin the lychees, cut them in half and remove the stones. Top and tail the mange-tout.
3. Blend the cornflour with the fruit juices and soy sauce. Stir the sugar into the cornflour mixture and put to one side.
4. Cut the pork into thin strips ½ × 3-inch (1.25 × 7.5-cm). Heat the oil in a saucepan, add the pork and stir-fry for 6–7 minutes or until cooked.
5. Boil about 2 pints (1.2 litres) water in a kettle.
6. Add the soy sauce mixture, lychees and mange-tout to the pork and stir-fry for 2–3 minutes.
7. Place the beansprouts in a saucepan, pour the boiling water over them and bring to the boil. Boil for 30–40 seconds and then drain.
8. Spoon the beansprouts onto four serving plates and top with the pork and lychees.

Selections per serving:
   1 Fat
   ½ Fruit
   3 Protein
   1¼ Vegetable
   15 Optional Calories

LIVER GRILL

SERVES 2

300 CALORIES PER SERVING

This simple recipe makes a quick and tasty meal.

1½oz (45g) breadcrumbs

1 teaspoon mixed herbs

¼ teaspoon powdered mustard

8oz (240g) lamb's liver, sliced

1½ teaspoons oil

3–4 slices onion

2 tomatoes, halved

4 large button mushrooms, halved

Tip:
Serve with stir-fried vegetables.

1. Mix together the breadcrumbs, herbs and mustard. Turn the slices of liver in the breadcrumbs and, using dry hands, press the breadcrumbs onto the liver.
2. Lay a piece of foil over a grill pan or baking sheet then brush it with ½ teaspoon of oil. Lay the liver on the foil.
3. Place the onion on the foil and brush with ½ teaspoon of oil.
4. Cook the liver and onion for 3–4 minutes under a preheated grill.
5. Remove the grill pan or baking sheet from the heat, turn the liver over and add the tomato halves and mushrooms. Brush the mushrooms with the remaining oil and return to the grill for a further 3–4 minutes – don't overcook or the liver will be tough.

Selections per serving:
¾ Bread
¾ Fat
3 Protein
1½ Vegetable

FISH CHOWDER

SERVES 4

215 CALORIES PER SERVING

This thick warming soup makes a delicious lunch or supper dish.

8oz (240g) smoked cod or haddock, skin removed

½ pint (300ml) skimmed milk

sprig of parsley

1 onion, finely chopped

2 teaspoons margarine

½ red pepper, seeded and chopped

4 teaspoons flour

6fl oz (180ml) vegetable stock

3oz (90g) drained canned sweetcorn

salt and pepper

2oz (60g) cooked ham, diced

4 tablespoons grated Parmesan cheese

Tip:
Serve with slices of French bread and follow with fresh fruit.

1. Place the smoked fish, milk, parsley and just under half of the onion in a saucepan. Cover and leave to simmer over a low heat for 8–10 minutes.
2. Heat the margarine in a separate saucepan, add the remaining onion and stir-fry for 1–2 minutes. Add the red pepper, stir round, then cover and leave over a low heat for 5–6 minutes.
3. Transfer the fish, milk, etc. to a liquidiser and process to a purée.
4. Stir the flour into the onion and red pepper, gradually blend in the stock and bring to the boil, stirring all the time.
5. Pour the fish purée into the saucepan, add the sweetcorn and season with salt and pepper. Stir in the ham and bring to the boil. Simmer for 2–3 minutes, stirring occasionally, then remove from the heat.
6. Stir half the cheese into the soup, ladle into four warm bowls and sprinkle with the remaining cheese.

Selections per serving:
¼ Bread
½ Fat
¼ Milk
2 Protein
¼ Vegetable
40 Optional Calories

ROLLED SOLE KEBABS

SERVES 4

200 CALORIES PER SERVING

The white and black skins have to be removed from the fish fillets so the skewer can easily secure them round the banana.

8 × 3oz (90g) sole or plaice fillets

2 small courgettes

1 teaspoon lemon juice

1½ medium bananas

2 teaspoons oil

4 lemon wedges

Tip:
When removing the skin from white fish, hold it down with a piece of kitchen paper to prevent it from slipping.

1. Carefully remove the black and white skins from the fish fillets. Cut each fillet in half lengthways.
2. Thickly slice the courgettes. Place the slices in boiling water, bring back to the boil and boil for 2 minutes then drain.
3. Lay the fish fillets with the skinned sides facing up. Sprinkle the lemon juice over the fillets.
4. Cut the bananas into sixteen slices, place one slice on each fillet and roll the fish round it. Thread the fish and courgettes onto four skewers.
5. Brush the kebabs with oil and grill under a moderate heat for 10–12 minutes, turning and brushing with the remaining oil every 3–4 minutes. Serve each kebab with a wedge of lemon.

Selections per serving:
½ Fat
¾ Fruit
4 Protein
½ Vegetable

PRAWNS IN FROMAGE FRAIS

SERVES 2

160 CALORIES PER SERVING

Be sure to stir the fromage frais while heating or it will curdle.

4oz (120g) small courgettes, sliced

2 teaspoons margarine

2 tablespoons chopped spring onions

2 teaspoons lemon juice

4oz (120g) prawns

2 teaspoons cornflour

4oz (120g) fromage frais

paprika

2 lemon wedges

Tip:
Use a heavy-based saucepan when making egg-based sauces or mixtures containing yogurt or fromage frais. This will help to prevent burning and curdling.

1. Blanch the courgette slices in boiling water for 1–1½ minutes and drain.
2. Melt the margarine in a saucepan, add the spring onions and stir-fry for 1–2 minutes. Remove from the heat then add the lemon juice and prawns.
3. Place the cornflour in a small bowl, gradually blend in the fromage frais, then stir into the saucepan with the prawn mixture and bring to the boil, stirring all the time. Remove from the heat.
4. Spoon the creamy prawns and courgettes mixture into a warm serving bowl, sprinkle with paprika and garnish with the lemon wedges.

Selections per serving:
1 Fat
3 Protein
¾ Vegetable
10 Optional Calories

BUCK RAREBIT

SERVES 2

325 CALORIES PER SERVING

The addition of salt to simmering water raises its boiling-point and the eggs therefore poach more quickly, helping to prevent the whites breaking up. Allow about 1 – 1 1/2 teaspoons salt to every 1/2 pint (300ml) water.

salt

2 × 1oz (30g) slices of bread

2 tablespoons skimmed milk or brown ale

3oz (90g) Cheddar cheese, grated

1/4 teaspoon mustard

2 eggs

Tip:
When poaching eggs in water, very gently stir the water to draw the white round the yolk.

1. Place a saucepan about a quarter full of hot salted water over a moderate heat while preparing the recipe.
2. Toast the bread in a toaster or under the grill.
3. Mix the milk or brown ale, cheese and mustard together in a very small heavy-based saucepan. Heat very gently, stirring all the time until the cheese has melted.
4. Spoon the melted cheese onto the hot toast and cook under a moderate grill until bubbling and golden.
5. Break the eggs one at a time into the simmering water and cook for about 3 minutes until the whites have set.
6. Place one slice of toast onto each serving plate, lift the poached eggs from the simmering water with a fish slice and lay one on top of each slice of toasted cheese.

Selections per serving:
1 Bread
2 1/2 Protein
5 Optional Calories

Toasted Sandwiches

TOASTED SANDWICHES

CHEESE AND ONION

SERVES 1

365 CALORIES PER SERVING

1½ teaspoons margarine

2 × 1oz (30g) slices of bread

1½oz (45g) slice of cheese or grated cheese

few onion rings

English or French mustard

Selections per serving:
  2 Bread
  1½ Fat
  1½ Protein

1. Spread half the margarine over one slice of bread, then lay it margarine side down on a sheet of foil.
2. Lay the slice of cheese on top of the dry side of the bread or scatter the grated cheese evenly on the bread. Arrange a few onion rings on top.
3. Spread a very thin layer of mustard on one side of the remaining slice of bread. Press the slice, mustard side down, over the cheese and onion.
4. Spread the remaining margarine over the top layer of bread.
5. Transfer the sandwich, on the foil, to a preheated grill and cook, turning once, until golden brown. Alternatively, cook in a sandwich toaster.

HAM AND TOMATO

SERVES 2

265 CALORIES PER SERVING

1 tablespoon margarine

4 × 1oz (30g) slices of bread

2 × 1½oz (45g) slices of cooked ham

1 tomato, sliced

English mustard

Selections per serving:
  2 Bread
  1½ Fat
  1½ Protein

1. Spread half the margarine over two slices of bread, then lay them margarine side down on a sheet of foil.
2. Lay one slice of ham on each piece of bread and arrange the slices of tomato on top.
3. Spread a thin layer of mustard over each of the remaining slices of bread. Press these slices, mustard side down, over the ham and tomato.
4. Spread the remaining margarine over the top layer of bread.
5. Transfer the sandwich, on the foil, to a preheated grill and cook, turning once, until golden. Alternatively, cook in a sandwich toaster.

 VEGETARIAN

BLUE CHEESE CRUNCH

SERVES 3

260 CALORIES PER SERVING

1oz (30g) Danish blue cheese

2oz (60g) curd cheese

½oz (15g) walnuts, chopped

½ medium apple, peeled, cored and chopped

1–2 teaspoons skimmed milk

6 × 1oz (30g) slices of bread

4½ teaspoons margarine

Tip:
Sandwich toasters require the margarine to be on the outside of the sandwich, but if the sandwich is to be grilled, margarine can be spread on the inner side.

1. Mash the Danish blue cheese in a small basin, mix in the curd cheese, walnuts and apple. Add sufficient milk to make a thick paste.
2. Spread three slices of bread with half the margarine. Place the bread, margarine side down on a sheet of foil.
3. Spread the blue cheese spread evenly over the three slices of bread, cover with the remaining bread and spread with the rest of the margarine.
4. Transfer the sandwiches and foil to a preheated grill and cook, turning once, until golden brown. Alternatively, cook in a sandwich toaster.

Selections per serving:
    2 Bread
    1½ Fat
    1 Protein
    20 Optional Calories

TACOS

SERVES 2

180 CALORIES PER SERVING

Taco shells are readily available now and, when filled, make a tasty snack meal. They are usually heated in a warm oven but this can be equally successfully carried out under a grill, thus saving time.

I tomato

2oz (60g) avocado

3oz (90g) cooked chicken

3–4 teaspoons finely chopped onion

good pinch of chilli powder

good pinch of salt

2 tablespoons low-fat natural yogurt

2 taco shells

shredded lettuce

> **Tip:**
> Always heat taco shells with a ball of foil in the middle – this will prevent the sides collapsing towards each other.

1. Cover the tomato with boiling water, leave for 30–40 seconds, then drain and slip off the skin.
2. Chop the tomato. Mash the avocado and stir in the tomato.
3. Chop the chicken and stir into the avocado mixture with the onion, chilli powder, salt and yogurt.
4. Crumple two pieces of foil and place one in each taco shell. Place under a moderately hot grill for one minute.
5. Spoon the avocado and chicken mixture into the taco shells and top with a little shredded lettuce.

Selections per serving:
I Bread
I Fat
I ½ Protein
½ Vegetable
I0 Optional Calories

TEMPEH STIR-FRY

SERVES 2

210 CALORIES PER SERVING

Tempeh is made by culturing freshly cooked soya beans. Unlike tofu, tempeh must be cooked before eating.

6oz (180g) tempeh, thawed

4½ teaspoons oil

½ small clove garlic

⅜-inch (1-cm) root ginger

4 spring onions, sliced

1 red pepper, cored, seeded and cut into 1½-inch (4-cm) pieces

1 courgette, cut into 1½-inch (4-cm) thin lengths

approximately 2 tablespoons soy sauce

3oz (90g) beansprouts

2 teaspoons pumpkin seeds

2 teaspoons sunflower seeds

Tip:
The grey or black patches on tempeh are normal – this does not indicate spoilage.

1. Cut the tempeh into slices ¼ × 2-inch (5-mm × 5-cm).
2. Heat 2 teaspoons of oil in a frying pan with a lid or a saucepan. Add half the tempeh and stir-fry until beginning to brown. Remove from the pan and add 1 teaspoon oil and the remaining tempeh and stir-fry until beginning to brown – if necessary add ½ teaspoon more oil. Transfer all the tempeh to a plate.
3. Finely chop the garlic. Peel the ginger, cut into very thin slices then cut each slice into three or four pieces.
4. Heat the remaining oil in the pan, add the garlic and ginger and stir-fry for a few seconds. Then add the spring onions, red pepper, courgette, 4 tablespoons water and 1 tablespoon soy sauce. Bring to the boil and boil rapidly for 2 minutes.
5. Stir the tempeh and beansprouts into the vegetables, cover and place over a moderate heat for 2 minutes. Stir in the seeds and season to taste with more soy sauce.

Selections per serving:
  2 Fat
  3 Protein
  1½ Vegetable
  50 Optional Calories

TUNA SALAD

SERVES 4

200 CALORIES PER SERVING

Serve this dish with a simple mixed salad.

15oz (450g) potatoes, cut into ½-inch (1.25-cm) cubes

salt

4oz (120g) dwarf beans, cut into 1-inch (2.5-cm) lengths

8 anchovy fillets plus 1 teaspoon of oil from the can

2 tablespoons low-calorie mayonnaise

4 tablespoons low-fat natural yogurt

6oz (180g) drained canned tuna

3 tomatoes

3-inch (7.5-cm) wedge cucumber

4 lemon wedges

Tip:
If possible use small new potatoes, which have a firm waxy texture.

1. Cook the potatoes in boiling salted water for about 12 minutes until firm but cooked, then drain.
2. Cook the beans in boiling salted water for 8–10 minutes, then drain.
3. Roughly chop the anchovies then, using a pestle and mortar, pound the anchovies and gradually mix in the mayonnaise. Alternatively mash the anchovies and gradually add the mayonnaise.
4. Stir the reserved oil from the can of anchovies and the yogurt into the anchovy mayonnaise.
5. Flake the tuna into large pieces and stir in the potato and beans. Spoon the anchovy dressing over the tuna salad and mix well.
6. Pile the tuna mixture onto a serving plate. Thinly slice the tomatoes and cucumber and arrange round the salad. Serve with lemon wedges.

Selections per serving:
   1 Bread
   1 Fat
   1½ Protein
   1¼ Vegetable
   40 Optional Calories

 VEGETARIAN

TOFU GRATINÉE

SERVES 2

300 CALORIES PER SERVING

Any variety of hard cheese may be used for this recipe but a fully matured Cheddar gives a good flavour.

1 teaspoon oil

1 clove garlic, chopped

1 onion, chopped

½ teaspoon chilli powder

½ teaspoon honey

1 small (8oz/227g) can chopped tomatoes

6oz (180g) tofu, cubed

6oz (180g) drained canned chick peas

1oz (30g) cheese

1oz (30g) fresh breadcrumbs

½oz (15g) peanuts

Tip:
Cover the remaining tofu with cold water and place in the refrigerator. If you wish to keep the tofu for a second day replace the cold water and leave in the refrigerator.

1. Heat the oil in a saucepan, add the garlic and onion and stir-fry for 5 minutes until the onion is translucent and soft.
2. Stir in the chilli powder, mix well, then stir in the honey, tomatoes, tofu and chick peas. Bring to the boil, stirring all the time, then cover the saucepan and simmer for 10–15 minutes, stirring occasionally.
3. Meanwhile finely grate the cheese and mix with the breadcrumbs. Chop the peanuts and mix into the breadcrumbs and cheese.
4. Spoon the vegetables into a flameproof serving dish, sprinkle with the breadcrumb mixture and brown under a hot grill.

Selections per serving:
  ½ Bread
  ¾ Fat
  3 Protein
  2 Vegetable
  5 Optional Calories

SCOTCH PANCAKES

SERVES 4

215 CALORIES PER SERVING

These pancakes may be served alone or spread with margarine but remember to adjust the Selections and calories.

salt

1 teaspoon oil

4oz (120g) self-raising flour

2 tablespoons caster sugar

1 egg

¼ pint (150ml) skimmed milk

8 teaspoons maple or golden syrup

Tip:
To prevent the syrup sticking to the teaspoon, lightly grease the spoon – it will then slip off the spoon in a continuous stream.

1. Prove a griddle or large frying pan: cover the base with a thin layer of salt and heat gently until the salt is very hot. Tip the salt out of the pan and rub all over the base with a double piece of kitchen paper. Allow to cool then brush a little oil over the surface.

2. Sieve the flour into a bowl, stir in the sugar and make a well in the centre. Break the egg into the well, add a little milk and beat until smooth. Gradually add all the milk to form a smooth batter.

3. Place the griddle over a moderate heat. When the griddle is hot either pour a little batter or spoon about a tablespoon of the batter to make several small pancakes. When bubbles begin to rise and set on each pancake use a palette knife to turn them over and cook until golden brown. Keep the pancakes warm by wrapping in a clean tea cloth while cooking the remaining batter. Add a little more oil to the griddle and repeat the procedure to make sixteen pancakes.

4. Arrange four pancakes on each warm serving plate, pour over the syrup and serve.

Selections per serving:
1 Bread
¼ Fat
¼ Protein
80 Optional Calories

BANANA MERINGUE

SERVES 4

190 CALORIES PER SERVING

This recipe is simple and quick. Cook it in a deep flameproof dish so the meringue completely covers the custard.

4 tablespoons custard powder

2½ teaspoons granulated sugar

1 pint (600ml) skimmed milk

finely grated zest of 1 lemon

3 medium bananas

1 large egg white

pinch of cream of tartar

2 tablespoons caster sugar

Tip:
Always add a pinch of cream of tartar when whisking egg whites; it helps to stabilise the foam.

1. Spoon the custard powder and granulated sugar into a jug and blend to a smooth paste with a little milk.
2. Heat the remaining milk and lemon zest in a saucepan until steaming, pour onto the custard powder mixture then return to the saucepan and bring to the boil, stirring all the time. Boil for 1 minute then remove from the heat.
3. Slice the bananas, stir into the custard and spoon into a deep flameproof dish.
4. Whisk the egg white with the cream of tartar until peaking, add half the caster sugar and whisk again until peaking, then repeat to incorporate the remaining sugar.
6. Pile the meringue on top of the hot custard. Draw up to form peaks then place under a moderately hot grill for 1½–2 minutes until golden.

Selections per serving:
    1½ Fruit
    ¼ Milk
    80 Optional Calories

EXOTIC SUNDAE

SERVES 3

180 CALORIES PER SERVING

A real treat made in just a few minutes.

1oz (30g) curd cheese

½oz (15g) fromage frais

1 medium banana

½ medium mango

1 kiwi fruit

2oz (60g) cherries, pineapple chunks or mandarins

6oz (180g) vanilla or chocolate ice cream

¼oz (10g) chocolate, grated

Tip:
Loosely cover the mango in a plastic bag and save for one or two days to make a recipe such as Tropical Mousse (p70).

1. Mix the curd cheese and fromage frais together until smooth. Cut the banana in half and mash one half to a smooth purée.
2. Prepare the mango by making three criss-cross cuts each way almost through to, but not through, the skin, then turn the outer edge under so the middle of the fruit rises and the flesh separates into about twelve pieces. Cut four or five cubes of mango from the skin and add to the banana purée.
3. Mash the two fruits together then gradually add to the curd cheese mixture. The fruits may be liquidised or sieved to make a smooth sauce but press firmly through the sieve or the purée will be too thin.
4. Cut the remaining mango from the skin and thickly slice the remaining banana and kiwi fruit. Mix all the fruits together then divide between three serving dishes.
5. Top each serving with ice cream, pour over the fruit and curd cheese sauce and sprinkle with grated chocolate. Serve immediately.

Selections per serving:
1½ Fruit
¼ Protein
115 Optional Calories

COOKING
FOR THE FREEZER

Freezers can be used to store pre-frozen food bought from shops but they are especially useful for storing high-quality seasonal produce, partially prepared foods and cooked dishes.

All food contains bacteria, and although freezing does not kill these microbes it prevents activity and they remain dormant. A refrigerator slows down the growth of bacteria and therefore stores most foods for short periods. Room and warm temperatures provide an ideal environment for the bacteria to multiply rapidly and food 'goes off' quickly. It is essential to cool food which is to be refrigerated or frozen very quickly. Food that is to be frozen must be rapidly cooled, chilled in a refrigerator and then frozen at a very low temperature. The lower the temperature the smaller the ice crystals will be. Ice crystals cause slight damage to food but if the fast freeze button is switched on several hours before freezing food, and is left on for several hours after it has been put in the cabinet, the crystals will be small and therefore cause minimum damage. If large quantities are to be frozen, stagger the time the food is put in the freezer and put the fast freeze button on about 12 hours before and 24 hours after placing in the cabinet.

There are many different types of freezer but they can be divided into three categories: combined fridge freezers, upright and chest models. The temperature of cabinets varies and, depending on their star rating, some so-called freezers are really only conserves, i.e. they store pre-frozen foods for limited periods. A single star is only suitable for safely storing pre-frozen food for one week, two stars for one month and three stars for three months. Four stars indicate that fresh food and prepared dishes can safely be frozen.

Although frozen food held at, or below, $-18°C$ ($0°F$) doesn't 'go off', its nature is affected and textures and flavours gradually alter. For example, tofu toughens and garlic dishes develop a musty flavour, while mushrooms go slimy. It is for this reason that foods have recommended storage times.

Packaging is important. It must always be moisture- and vapour-proof. Suitable containers include some waxed card containers, very thick foil, polythene bags which must be sealed with freezer tape or ties and plastic boxes with tightly fitting lids. As food slightly increases in volume during freezing due to the formation of ice crystals, allow a ½-inch (1.25-cm) space between the food and container lid. Label clearly with date, contents and portion size. A waterproof felt-tip pen or chinagraph pencil should be used so the information does not get wiped off. Always label prior to freezing otherwise the label will not remain in place. Different coloured labels are useful: specific colours can be used for particular foods, such as blue for fish, green for vegetables and so on.

Freezers are usually reliable but they are affected by some factors. They should never be moved more than 30 degrees so make sure care is taken when moving from one position to another. This is particularly important when moving house.

Power cuts can cause many problems but, if certain precautions are taken, they need not result in a disaster. Never open the freezer door during the cut. Immediately power is restored switch on the fast freeze button. If you are given advance warning switch the fast freeze button on about eight hours before the power cut is to take effect. When possible cover the freezer with a thick blanket or rug. If these instructions are followed food should remain safely frozen for about ten hours.

FREEZER FACTS

FOOD	RECOMMENDED MAXIMUM STORAGE TIME
Baked	
Biscuits – cooked and uncooked	3 months
Bread – cooked	2 weeks
Cakes – cooked	3 months
Scones – cooked	3 months
Cheese (cottage cheese is unsuitable)	3 months
Fish – uncooked	
White e.g. cod, haddock	3 months
Oily e.g. herring, salmon	2 months
Fish – cooked	
White and oily	2 months
Shellfish	1 month
Meat – uncooked	
Beef	8 months
Lamb	6 months
Offal	3 months
Minced beef, lamb, pork	3 months
Pork	6 months
Sausages	1 month
Veal	3 months
Meat – cooked	
Casseroles, goulashes, curries	2 months
Pâtés, terrines, loaves	1 month
Poultry – uncooked	
Chicken	12 months
Turkey	6 months
Poultry – cooked	
Casseroles, curries	2 months
Herbs	6 months

All recipes marked * are suitable for vegetarians as well as non-vegetarians

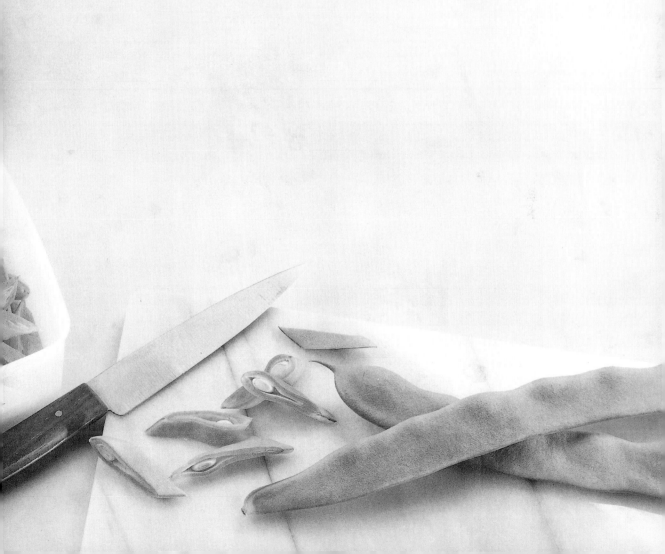

COURGETTE AND MINT SOUP

SERVES 6

50 CALORIES PER SERVING

It's useful to have any kind of soup in the freezer but soup which is served chilled is a real advantage. Leave the soup to thaw then stir in the milk and it's ready.

2 teaspoons margarine

I onion, chopped

3oz (90g) potato, diced

Ilb (480g) courgettes, chopped

¾ pint (450ml) vegetable stock

I tablespoon very finely chopped mint

To serve:

¼ pint (150ml) skimmed milk

salt and pepper

Freezer Notes:
Storage 3 months

1. Melt the margarine, add the chopped onion and stir-fry for 4–5 minutes.
2. Stir the potato, courgettes, stock and mint into the saucepan and bring to the boil. Cover and simmer for 25–30 minutes.
3. Pour the soup into a food processor or blender and process for a few seconds or until smooth.
4. Allow to cool then pour the soup into a suitable container and freeze.

To serve: Leave the soup to thaw, stir in the milk and season to taste with salt and pepper.

Selections per serving:
¼ Fat
I Vegetable
30 Optional Calories

CREAM OF CELERY SOUP

SERVES 6

60 CALORIES PER SERVING

It's surprising how much the weight of celery heads varies. If I'm in a supermarket I weigh them to make sure I get my money's worth!

1 head celery (approx. 1lb (480g) trimmed weight)

1 large onion

6oz (180g) potatoes

¾ pint (450ml) vegetable stock

To serve:

¼ pint (150ml) whole milk

grated nutmeg

salt and pepper

3 tablespoons single cream

Freezer Notes:
Storage 3 months

1. Roughly chop the celery, celery leaves, onion and potato. Place the vegetables and stock in a saucepan, cover and simmer for 25 minutes.
2. Pour the vegetables and stock into a food processor or blender and process to a purée.
3. Transfer the purée to a suitable container, cool and freeze.

To serve: Leave to thaw, place the purée in a saucepan and stir in the milk. Season well with the nutmeg, salt and pepper. Bring to the boil, simmer for 3–4 minutes, then pour into warm soup bowls and swirl in the cream.

Selections per serving:
   ¼ Bread
   1¼ Vegetable
   45 Optional Calories

TANGY CRUSH

SERVES 6

50 CALORIES PER SERVING

This is a refreshing cold starter ideal for a hot summer's day. Serve when the tiny ice crystals are just beginning to form.

24fl oz (720ml) tomato and vegetable juice

2 medium oranges

1 small onion

3–4 sprigs of basil

2 teaspoons sugar

Freezer Notes:
Storage 6 months

1. Pour the tomato and vegetable juice into a saucepan.
2. Remove the zest from one orange using a potato peeler. Squeeze the juice from both the oranges.
3. Chop the onion and place the onion, orange zest and juice and basil into the saucepan. Cover and simmer gently for 15 minutes then remove from the heat, stir in the sugar and leave until cool.
4. Sieve the tomato juice etc. into a container and freeze until firm, though not completely hard.

To serve: If the crush is to be served the same day, as soon as it is firm transfer to a plastic bag and tap with a rolling pin to reduce to small ice crystals. If the crush is to be served at a later date, remove from the freezer and leave until a knife will just go through the mixture, then proceed as described above.

Selections per serving:
¾ Fruit
10 Optional Calories

BANGERS AND BEANS

SERVES 4

255 CALORIES PER SERVING

This recipe uses canned beans but canned chick peas may be used in their place.

8oz (240g) pork and beef chipolata sausages

2 × 1oz (30g) rashers lean back bacon, rind removed

1 teaspoon oil

1 onion, roughly chopped

1 small green pepper, seeded and roughly chopped

1 small (8oz/227g) can chopped tomatoes

dash of hot pepper sauce

4fl oz (120ml) vegetable stock

6oz (180g) drained canned haricot or borletti beans

Freezer Notes:
Storage 2 months

1. Twist the sausages in half and grill until the fat stops dripping from them and they are lightly browned or grill them whole, then cut in half. Grill the bacon until the fat stops dripping from it then cut into ½-inch (1.25-cm) strips.
2. Heat the oil in a saucepan. Add the onion and pepper and stir-fry for 5 minutes.
3. Stir the tomatoes, hot pepper sauce, stock, beans, sausages and bacon into the saucepan and bring to the boil over a low heat. Cover the saucepan and leave to simmer for 20 minutes, stirring from time to time. Cool, then freeze rapidly.

To serve: Leave to thaw, place in a saucepan, cover and simmer for 10 minutes, stirring occasionally.

Selections per serving:
¼ Fat
3 Protein
1 Vegetable

BEEF IN GRAPE JUICE

SERVES 4

275 CALORIES PER SERVING

This dish makes a tasty meal suitable for the family or when entertaining guests.

1lb (480g) braising steak

1 clove garlic

6 juniper berries, crushed

16fl oz (480ml) red grape juice

1 large onion, thinly sliced

1 tablespoon margarine

1 tablespoon flour

1 bulb fennel, thinly sliced

bouquet garni

Freezer Notes:
Storage 2 months

1. Lay the braising steak in a non-metallic container. Add a whole peeled clove of garlic, juniper berries, 8fl oz (240ml) grape juice and a slice of onion. Leave in the refrigerator for several hours or overnight.
2. Remove the braising steak from the marinade and lay it on the rack of a grill pan. Grill under a low to moderate heat, turning once, until the fat stops dripping from the meat. Allow to cool then cut into four pieces.
3. Heat the margarine in a flameproof casserole dish. Add the remaining onion and stir-fry for 2 minutes until limp. Sprinkle the flour over the onion and stir well. Gradually add the remaining grape juice. Remove the garlic from the marinade then stir into the casserole. Bring to the boil over a moderate heat then stir in the fennel and bouquet garni.
4. Remove the casserole from the heat and lay the beef on top of the vegetables. Push the beef down so it is covered by the grape juice.
5. Transfer the casserole to the oven set at 325°F, 160°C, Gas Mark 3 and cook for 1¾ hours.
6. Cool rapidly, transfer to a suitable container and freeze.

To serve: Thaw the beef and grape juice, pour into a saucepan and place over a moderate heat. Bring to the boil, cover and simmer gently for 5–10 minutes. Remove the bouquet garni and serve.

Selections per serving:
¾ Fat
1 Fruit
3 Protein
¾ Vegetable
10 Optional Calories

FISH CAKES WITH TOMATO SAUCE

SERVES 4

340 CALORIES PER SERVING

This is really two recipes in one. The tomato sauce tastes best if it is made with very ripe, sweet tomatoes.

For the fish cakes:

12oz (360g) potatoes

salt

11oz (330g) well drained canned pilchards (you will need a 425g can for this quantity)

1 egg

3 tablespoons skimmed milk

2½oz (75g) dry breadcrumbs

2 tablespoons oil

For the tomato sauce:

12oz (360g) tomatoes, quartered

1 carrot, roughly chopped

1 stick celery, roughly chopped

½ medium onion, roughly chopped

sprig of basil

one large pinch of chilli powder

Selections per serving:
  1½ Bread
  1½ Fat
  3 Protein
  1½ Vegetable
  15 Optional Calories

To make the fish cakes:
1. Boil the potatoes in salted water until cooked, drain very well, then mash.
2. Mash the pilchards and potatoes together.
3. Lightly beat the egg and milk together, reserve 4 tablespoons and gradually mix the remainder into the pilchards and potatoes.
4. Divide the mixture into eight and shape into fish cakes. Refrigerate the fish cakes for 20–30 minutes.
5. Pour the remaining egg and milk mixture onto one plate and the breadcrumbs onto another. Turn each fish cake in the egg and then the breadcrumbs so they are evenly coated.
6. Heat the oil in a frying pan and cook the fish cakes, three or four at a time, until golden on each side. Cool the fish cakes then open freeze before packing in a suitable container.

To make the tomato sauce:
1. Place all the ingredients in a saucepan, cover tightly and place over a low heat. Leave to simmer for about 45 minutes.
2. Transfer the hot tomato mixture to a food processor or liquidiser. Process for a few seconds then press through a sieve. Cool rapidly then freeze.

To serve: Place the frozen fish cakes on a baking sheet lined with non-stick baking parchment. Bake in a preheated oven at 400°F, 200°C, Gas Mark 6 for about 35 minutes until heated through. Leave the sauce to thaw, pour into a small saucepan and reheat, stirring all the time.

Freezer Notes:
Storage 2 months

LASAGNE

SERVES 6

360 CALORIES PER SERVING

Allow plenty of time for the Lasagne to thaw. The colder it is, the longer it will take to cook.

1lb 4oz (600g) minced beef

1 teaspoon oil

1 large onion, chopped

8oz (240g) mixture of carrot and swede, diced

1 small (8oz/227g) can chopped tomatoes

¼ pint (150ml) vegetable or beef stock

1½oz (45g) plus 2 teaspoons cornflour

½ teaspoon marjoram

1 tablespoon margarine

¾ pint (450ml) skimmed milk

4 oz (120g) cheese, grated

6oz (180g) precooked lasagne (9 sheets)

Freezer Notes:
Storage 2 months

Selections per serving:
1¼ Bread
½ Fat
¼ Milk
3½ Protein
¾ Vegetable
10 Optional Calories

1. Shape the minced beef into small patties, lay on the rack of a grill pan and grill, turning once, until the fat stops dripping from the meat.
2. Heat the oil in a saucepan, add the onion and stir-fry for 3–4 minutes. Crumble the minced beef into the saucepan, stir in the carrot, swede and tomatoes.
3. Blend a little stock with 2 teaspoons of cornflour and put to one side. Stir the remaining stock and marjoram into the saucepan, bring to the boil and simmer for 20–25 minutes. Stir in the cornflour paste and return to the boil, stirring all the time. Boil for 1 minute then remove from the heat.
4. Melt the margarine in a separate saucepan, remove from the heat, add the remaining cornflour and stir well, gradually blend in the milk then return to the heat. Bring to the boil, stirring continuously. Boil for 2 minutes then remove from the heat.
5. Reserve ½–1oz (15–30g) cheese and stir the remainder into the white sauce.
6. Line a dish with large sheets of double thickness foil so it extends well over each side of the dish. Spread about a quarter of the cheese sauce over the base, lay three sheets of pasta on the sauce, then top with a layer of about half the meat sauce. Cover with three more sheets of pasta and the remaining meat sauce. Complete with the remaining sheets of pasta and spread the remaining cheese sauce evenly over the top.
7. Sprinkle the cheese over, cool rapidly, then freeze. Freeze for about an hour until firm then, using the foil edges, lift out of the dish, cover with the foil and place in a suitable container and return to the freezer.

To serve: Allow plenty of time for the Lasagne to thaw. Carefully remove the foil while frozen and transfer to a dish. Place in a preheated oven at 375°F, 190°C, Gas Mark 5 for 45–50 minutes. Brown under a hot grill.

SEAMAN'S STEW

SERVES 4

175 CALORIES PER SERVING

This recipe uses a combination of firm-fleshed fish so their shape and texture is maintained throughout cooking, freezing and reheating. If you prefer you can use only one type of the listed fish.

1 tablespoon olive oil

1 clove garlic, chopped

1 large leek, thickly sliced

½ green pepper, seeded and cut into ½-inch (1.25-cm) squares

2 sticks celery, sliced

1 small (8oz/227g) can chopped tomatoes

3oz (90g) baby corn on the cob cut in ½-inch (1.25-cm) slices

4fl oz (120ml) white wine

½ teaspoon of fennel seeds

4 tablespoons weak stock

1lb (480g) mixture of boneless monkfish, red mullet and huss

Freezer Notes:
Storage 2 months

1. Heat the oil in a saucepan, add the garlic and leek and stir-fry for 3 minutes. Add the pepper and celery and stir-fry for 1 minute, then cover the saucepan, reduce the heat to as low as possible and leave to cook for 4 minutes.
2. Stir the tomatoes, corn and wine into the saucepan, add the fennel seeds and stock. Cover the saucepan and simmer for 15–20 minutes.
3. Cut the fish into large pieces about 2-inches (5-cm) square. Stir the fish into the vegetables, cover and simmer gently for 12 minutes until just cooked.
4. Quickly cool, transfer to a suitable container and freeze.

To serve: Thaw the stew, place in a saucepan, cover and slowly bring to the boil. Simmer for 5 minutes.

Selections per serving:
¼ Bread
¾ Fat
3½ Protein
1½ Vegetable
30 Optional Calories

STRAWBERRY CURD TART

SERVES 8

220 CALORIES PER SERVING

The strawberries may be substituted with other fresh fruit.

4½oz (135g) plain flour plus 2 teaspoons for rolling pastry

pinch of salt

4 tablespoons margarine

approximately 4 teaspoons ice-cold water

8oz (240g) curd cheese

4 teaspoons caster sugar

2 eggs, beaten

5fl oz (150ml) low-fat natural yogurt

finely grated zest of ¼ of a medium orange

To serve:

8oz (240g) strawberries

3 tablespoons sieved strawberry jam

Selections per serving:
    ½ Bread
    1½ Fat
    ¾ Protein
    60 Optional Calories

1. Sieve 4½oz (135g) of flour and the salt into a bowl. Add the margarine (if possible margarine which has been stored in the freezer). Rub the margarine into the flour until the mixture resembles fresh breadcrumbs.
2. Using a round-bladed knife mix the cold water into the flour and margarine to form a dough. If time allows, wrap the pastry and chill for 20–30 minutes.
3. Dust a sheet of non-stick baking parchment and the rolling pin with a little of the remaining flour. Roll out and line a 7½-inch (19-cm) fluted flan tin, dusting the pastry with the remaining flour when necessary.
4. Press the pastry sides firmly, trim the edge and prick the base with a fork. Lay a piece of baking parchment in the flan and weigh it down with a few dried beans or rice. Bake at 400°F, 200°C, Gas Mark 6 for 10 minutes then remove the parchment and beans and cook for a further 5 minutes.
5. Mix the curd cheese and sugar together. Gradually add the beaten eggs then stir in the yogurt and orange zest. Spoon the curd cheese mixture into the hot flan case and return to the oven at 325°F, 160°C, Gas Mark 3 for 25–30 minutes or until set. Leave to cool.

To serve: Lay the tart on a cooling rack and leave to thaw then slide it carefully onto a flat serving plate. Halve the strawberries and arrange on top of the cold curd tart. Warm the jam and brush over the strawberries and the top of the tart.

Freezer Notes:
Storage 3 months

Strawberry Curd Tart

 VEGETARIAN

APPLE AND PLUM PUDDING

SERVES 4

275 CALORIES PER SERVING

This pudding can be cooked, frozen and then thawed and eaten cold or reheated. Alternatively it may be assembled, frozen and cooked when thawed. Either way it must be completely thawed or it will remain cold in the centre after cooking.

2lbs (1kg) mixture of sweet plums and cooking apples

4 teaspoons sugar

3oz (90g) plain flour

¼ teaspoon allspice

2 tablespoons margarine

1½oz (45g) ground almonds

Freezer Notes:
Storage 2 months

1. Stone the plums and cut into quarters. Peel, quarter and core the apples, then cut each piece in half. Place the fruit in a saucepan, add 1 tablespoon of water, cover and leave over a very low heat until the fruit is half cooked. Sweeten with 2 teaspoons of sugar – if the plums are a little tart add a little artificial sweetener.

2. Sieve the flour and allspice. Rub in the margarine (if possible margarine that has been stored in the freezer) until the mixture resembles fresh breadcrumbs.

3. Stir the remaining sugar and ground almonds into the flour.

4. Spoon the fruit into a very deep 6-inch (15-cm) ovenproof dish. Sprinkle the almond topping evenly over the fruit, leave until the fruit is completely cold, then freeze, or bake at 400°F, 200°C, Gas Mark 6 for 25 minutes, then cool and freeze.

To serve: Thaw uncovered, reheat at 300°F, 150°C, Gas Mark 3 for 30 minutes or cook at 400°F, 200°C, Gas Mark 6 for 30 minutes.

Selections per serving:
¾ Bread
1¾ Fat
2 Fruit
¾ Protein
30 Optional Calories

SCONE PIZZA

SERVES 6

240 CALORIES PER SERVING

This scone based pizza is much quicker to make than the bread based variety.

6oz (180g) plain flour

pinch of salt

pinch of powdered mustard

2 teaspoons baking powder

2 tablespoons margarine

1½oz (45g) cheese, finely grated

7 tablespoons skimmed milk

1½ teaspoons oil

1 medium onion, sliced

1 small green pepper, cored and thinly sliced

8oz (240g) tomatoes, skinned and chopped

¼ teaspoon oregano

4 anchovy fillets, chopped

1½ teaspoons tomato purée

½ teaspoon garlic purée

To serve:

3oz (90g) mozzarella cheese, thinly sliced

Selections per serving:
1 Bread
1¼ Fat
¾ Protein
½ Vegetable
10 Optional Calories

1. Reserve a teaspoon of flour. Sieve the remaining flour, salt, mustard and baking powder into a bowl.
2. Add the margarine (if possible margarine that has been stored in the freezer) and rub in until the mixture resembles fresh breadcrumbs. Stir in the grated cheese.
3. Make a well in the centre of the flour and pour in most of the milk. Using a round-bladed knife mix to form a soft dough gradually adding the remaining milk.
4. Sprinkle the work surface and rolling pin with the reserved flour and roll out the dough to form a circle 8 inches (20cm) in diameter.
5. Line a baking sheet with non-stick baking parchment. Transfer the dough to the baking sheet and leave at room temperature for 10–15 minutes, then bake at 450°F, 230°C, Gas Mark 8 for 8–9 minutes until cooked and beginning to brown.
6. While the dough is resting heat the oil in a frying pan. Add the onion and pepper and stir-fry for 4 minutes. Stir in the tomatoes and oregano and cook over a moderate heat for 10 minutes, then increase the heat and stir until the moisture has evaporated. Add the chopped anchovy fillets.
7. Mix the tomato and garlic purée together and spread thinly over the scone base. Spoon the onion and pepper mixture evenly on top. Open freeze the pizza then wrap in foil or transfer to a suitable container.

To serve: Remove from the foil or container, leave to thaw completely then wrap loosely in foil and reheat at 400°F, 200°C, Gas Mark 6 for 10–15 minutes. Remove from the oven, arrange the mozzarella over the top and grill under a moderate heat until the cheese has melted.

Freezer Notes:
Storage 3 months

COFFEE FLAN

SERVES 10

220 CALORIES PER SERVING

To make this recipe for a vegetarian, substitute the gelatine with a vegetable-based gelling agent.

1¾oz (50g) chocolate

7½ teaspoons margarine

10 large digestive biscuits

3 tablespoons water

1½ tablespoons instant coffee granules

1 sachet gelatine

12oz (360g) curd cheese

4oz (120g) fromage frais

5 tablespoons caster sugar

¼ pint (150ml) skimmed milk plus ½ teaspoon

Freezer notes:
Storage 2 months.

1. Break the chocolate into small pieces, reserve about ¼oz (10g) and place the remainder in a large basin. Place over a saucepan of simmering water and leave until melted.
2. Stir the margarine into the chocolate and leave until melted. If necessary replace over a saucepan of simmering water.
3. Crush the biscuits to form crumbs, add to the melted chocolate and stir well to coat. Spoon into an 8-inch (20-cm) springform or loose-bottomed cake tin and press the crumbs evenly over the base.
4. Measure the hot water into a small basin. Stir in the coffee granules and gelatine. Place in a saucepan of simmering water until dissolved.
5. Mix the curd cheese, fromage frais and sugar together, then gradually stir in ¼ pint (150ml) skimmed milk. Stir in the dissolved gelatine and pour over the chocolate crumb base. Leave until beginning to set.
6. Place the reserved chocolate and milk in a cup or small basin and stand in a saucepan of simmering water until the chocolate has dissolved. Stir well to mix the chocolate and milk then dip the prongs of a fork in the chocolate and run over the top of the coffee flan. Chill until completely set then remove from the tin and open freeze, then transfer to a suitable container and return to the freezer.

To serve:
Slide the flan onto a serving plate and leave until completely thawed before serving.

Selections per serving:
1 Bread
¾ Fat
¾ Protein
60 Optional Calories

Coffee Flan

ICE CREAM CAKE

SERVES 8

195 CALORIES PER SERVING

This cake is a real treat. The sorbet darkens a little during freezing but this doesn't affect the flavour.

For the sponge:

2 large eggs

4 tablespoons caster sugar

finely grated zest of 1 medium orange

2oz (60g) plain flour, sieved twice

For the syrup:

2 tablespoons concentrated frozen orange juice, thawed

2 tablespoons water

2 tablespoons sugar

1 tablespoon kirsch

For the cream sorbet:

8oz (240g) fresh or frozen raspberries or blackberries or a mixture

6 tablespoons single cream

6fl oz (180ml) water

8 tablespoons caster sugar

2 large egg whites

pinch of cream of tartar

2 tablespoons kirsch

To serve:

A few extra berries

3 kiwi fruits, sliced

1. Line an 8-inch (20-cm) sandwich tin with non-stick baking parchment – make sure the paper round the side tucks under the base and is about ½–1 inch (1.25cm–2.5cm) above the tin.

2. Place the eggs, sugar and orange zest in a bowl resting on a saucepan of simmering water. Using an electric mixer whisk the mixture until it is pale and thick – it should leave a trail when the whisk is raised. Remove from the heat and whisk for 2–3 minutes. Carefully fold in the flour and spoon into the prepared tin, tilting it slightly to level the surface. Bake at 350°F, 180°C, Gas Mark 4 until golden and just firm to the touch. Leave in the tin while preparing the syrup.

3. Place the orange juice, water and sugar in a small saucepan, heat gently until the sugar has dissolved, then increase the heat and boil for 30–40 seconds. Remove from the heat, allow to cool for a few seconds, then stir in the kirsch.

4. Using a skewer carefully make several holes through the surface of the sponge and spoon over about a tablespoon of the syrup, dribbling it evenly over the cake. Add the remaining syrup a little at a time. The cake may sink a little in the centre.

5. Prepare the cream sorbet: sieve the berries, pushing very hard against the sieve to extract as much juice as possible. Stir the cream into the purée and pour into a freezerproof container. Place the water and sugar in a small saucepan and heat gently until the sugar has dissolved, then increase the heat and boil for 3 minutes. Pour into the purée.

6. Carefully lift the sponge from the tin using the paper at the sides, then peel off the paper base and place on a flat freezerproof plate about 3 inches (7.5cm) larger than the sponge. Transfer the sponge to the freezer.

7. Freeze the sorbet until almost frozen, remove from the freezer and whisk with an electric mixer until thick. In a separate bowl whisk the egg

Freezer Notes:
Storage 3 months

whites and cream of tartar. Add the kirsch and whisk again until peaking. Quickly, but carefully, fold the egg whites into the purée, remove the cake from the freezer and pile the cream sorbet on top. Draw the sorbet up into peaks, allowing it to drop over the sides of the sponge. Open freeze for about 3 hours. When completely frozen, transfer to a large container to freeze until required.

To serve: Remove the plate from the freezer, scatter the berries between the peaks of the cream sorbet and arrange the kiwi fruit round the sides. Cut in slices and ease off the plate using a palette knife. Serve immediately.

Selections per serving:
¼ Bread
¾ Fruit
¼ Protein
135 Optional Calories

TOMATO PURÉE

10 CALORIES PER CUBE (APPROXIMATELY)

Every summer tomatoes become fairly cheap and, if you grow them, there is a sudden glut. Although they can be frozen whole then added to stews during the year, this purée is easy to make and it requires very little space for storage.

approximately 3lbs (1.5kg) tomatoes

a fresh bouquet garni of:
1 bay leaf
1 sprig parsley
1 sprig marjoram
1 sprig basil

Freezer Notes:
Storage 8 months

1. Cut the tomatoes in half or quarter them, depending on their size. Place in a large saucepan without any liquid. Cover and cook over a very low heat for about 30 minutes until soft.
2. Sieve the tomatoes, pressing hard against the sieve to extract as much juice as possible.
3. Pour the tomato juice into a clean saucepan. Tie the herbs together and add to the juice. Cook over a low heat, stirring occasionally, until reduced to ¾ pint (450ml) or less.
4. Remove the herbs from the purée – don't worry if a few leaves have broken off the sprigs and almost disintegrated as these can remain in the purée. Spoon into 12–16 divisions of an ice-cube tray.
5. Cool the cubes then freeze until solid. Pop the cubes out of the tray and pack in a bag or suitable container.

To use: Place a cube of purée while frozen into casseroles, stews etc. Alternatively, thaw and add to stir-fries and so on.

Selections per cube:
10 Optional Calories

COOKING
WITH A MICROWAVE

A microwave is one of the kitchen's greatest assets but, like any appliance, it must be used with care. Its method of cooking is very different from a conventional oven. A magnetron emits electromagnetic waves which penetrate approximately 2 inches (5cm) of the food, and these waves cause the molecules present in all foods and drinks to vibrate. This vibration results in heat which cooks the food.

Only 'microwave safe' containers should be used in the oven. These dishes are guaranteed not to contain metal which would deflect the electromagnetic waves. Many types of china and glass may be safely used but never cook in bone china or delicate or cut glass. Aluminium foil must *never* be used to cover the food totally, but can be used unless it is contrary to manufacturer's instructions, in very small quantities, to shield delicate areas such as fish tails which may be overcooked if left uncovered. The foil should never touch the walls of the oven. It should always be smooth and the shiny surface facing *inwards*. Never use the foil wrappings from bars of chocolate etc., or use metal ties to seal bags.

The following recipes have been tested in a 650 watt oven but if you have a microwave of different wattage use this chart as a guide:

500 watt add 20 seconds per minute   *700 watt deduct 10 seconds per minute*
600 watt add 10 seconds per minute

Please note that cooking times will vary from one oven to another and the voltage varies considerably from time to time, so use cooking times only as a guide. Undercook rather than overcook a recipe and let it stand for the recommended time then, if necessary, replace in the oven and cook for a little longer. Most models have inbuilt turntables but food may still need to be rearranged during cooking. If you own an oven which does not have a turntable refer to the manufacturer's instructions for a guide to the frequency with which food should be turned.

The power levels used in this section have been divided into three:

HIGH – approximately 100% power
MEDIUM – approximately 50% power
LOW – approximately 30% power

Unless otherwise stated food, except for sauces and liquids, should always be covered with a lid or upturned basin. If a recipe says to 'tightly cover' use either microwave clingfilm or a roasting bag. Do not stretch clingfilm when covering a dish and take care when removing it as the steam can easily cause scalds.

Conventional cooking methods have been included for most recipes to enable those who do not own microwave ovens to use this chapter.

All recipes marked * are suitable for vegetarians as well as non-vegetarians

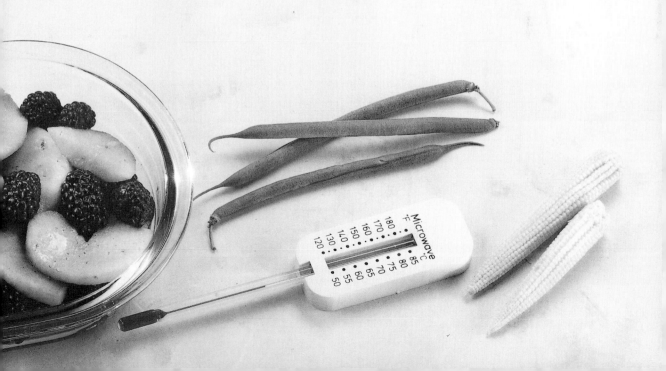

SIMPLE SOLO SUPPER

SERVES 1

185 CALORIES PER SERVING

This very simple recipe illustrates two of the microwave's advantages: a quick way of cooking fish that retains its texture and flavour.

1 medium leek

4oz (120g) cod or haddock fillet

½oz (15g) cheese, grated

½ tomato

Tip:
Always remove clingfilm carefully. Lift the side furthest from you back on itself so the steam doesn't rise over your arms.

1. Cut the leek in half lengthways. Cut each half into 3-inch (7.5-cm) lengths.
2. Place the leek and 4 tablespoons of water in a suitable container. Cover and microwave on HIGH for 3 minutes. Leave to stand for 1 minute, then drain well and transfer to the serving plate.
3. Lay the fish on top of the leeks. Cover tightly with clingfilm and cook on HIGH for 2 minutes.
4. Leave to stand for 1–2 minutes then carefully remove the clingfilm, lifting the side furthest from you to allow the steam to escape.
5. Sprinkle the grated cheese over the fish and decorate with tomato wedges or slices. Return to the microwave and cook on HIGH for 40 seconds.

Selections per serving:
3½ Protein
1½ Vegetable

SIMPLE SOLO SUPPER

SERVES 1

220 CALORIES PER SERVING

Don't use a large saucepan for this recipe, choose a heavy-based one which is just wide enough to hold the fish.

I medium leek

I teaspoon margarine

I tablespoon water or weak stock

4oz (120g) cod or haddock fillet

salt and pepper

½oz (15g) cheese, grated

½ tomato

1. Thinly slice the leek.
2. Melt the margarine in a small saucepan, add the leek and stir-fry for 1–2 minutes. Cover the saucepan and leave over a low heat for 4 minutes.
3. Stir the water or stock into the saucepan, lay the fish on top of the leeks and season with salt and pepper. Cover the saucepan and leave over a low heat for 8–10 minutes until the fish is just cooked.
4. Transfer the leeks, fish and the small amount of liquor to a flameproof dish.
5. Sprinkle the grated cheese over the fish. Slice or quarter the tomato and arrange round the edge of the dish. Place under a hot grill for 1–2 minutes until the cheese is bubbling.

Selections per serving:
I Fat
3½ Protein
1½ Vegetable
5 Optional Calories

TROUT WITH ASPARAGUS SAUCE

SERVES 2

200 CALORIES PER SERVING

Take care when using aluminium foil in a microwave. It must not touch the base or sides of the oven.

3oz (90g) drained canned asparagus

3 tablespoons single cream

3 small sprigs of mint

2 × 4oz (120g) trout fillets

lemon juice

2 lemon wedges

Tip:
Always use foil with the shiny side facing inwards.

1. Place the asparagus, cream and one sprig of mint in a blender and process until smooth. Pour the sauce into a bowl and put to one side.
2. Lay the trout fillets on a plate, protecting the tail end of each fillet with a small piece of foil. Cover the plate tightly with clingfilm and microwave on HIGH for 2 minutes. Leave to stand while heating the sauce.
3. Heat the asparagus sauce on HIGH for 1 minute, stirring halfway through the cooking time. Add lemon juice to taste.
4. Transfer the trout fillets to the serving plates. Stir any liquor from the fish into the sauce and spoon over each fillet. Garnish each serving with a sprig of mint and a wedge of lemon.

Selections per serving:
 3 Protein
 ½ Vegetable
 50 Optional Calories

TROUT WITH ASPARAGUS SAUCE

SERVES 2

225 CALORIES PER SERVING

To make such a small quantity of sauce requires considerable care so use a very small saucepan and stir continuously.

2 × 4oz (120g) trout fillets

1½ teaspoons margarine

3oz (90g) drained canned asparagus

3 tablespoons single cream

3 small sprigs of mint

lemon juice

2 lemon wedges

1. Lay a piece of foil on top of the rack of a grill pan and place the trout fillets on top, skin side down. Dot the fish with the margarine and put to one side.
2. Place the asparagus, cream and one sprig of mint in the goblet of a blender and process until smooth.
3. Cook the trout under a moderate grill for about 4 minutes. There is no need to turn the fish as the fillets are very thin.
4. While the trout is cooking heat the asparagus sauce in a very small saucepan, stirring all the time. Add the lemon juice to taste.
5. Transfer the trout fillets to two warm serving plates. Mix any of the trout juices remaining on the foil into the sauce, stir well and spoon over each fillet. Garnish each serving with a sprig of mint and a wedge of lemon. Serve immediately.

Selections per serving:
¾ Fat
3 Protein
½ Vegetable
50 Optional Calories

PASTA RATATOUILLE

SERVES 3

305 CALORIES PER SERVING

This variation of a ratatouille makes a filling snack meal.

6oz (180g) aubergine

salt

1 onion, chopped

1 clove garlic, finely chopped

1 medium (15oz/497g) can chopped tomatoes

1 tablespoon tomato purée

4 tablespoons water or vegetable stock

3oz (90g) pasta spirals

9oz (270g) tofu, cut in ½-inch (1.25-cm) cubes

1 large green pepper, seeded and cut into ½-inch (1.25-cm) squares

12oz (360g) mixture drained canned kidney and flageolet beans

Tip:
If you are particularly fond of garlic, increase the quantity to one large or two small cloves.

1. Cut the aubergine into 1-inch (2.5-cm) cubes, place in a sieve and sprinkle with salt. Leave for 30 minutes to allow the bitter juices to drip out, then rinse well.
2. Place the onion, garlic and chopped tomatoes in a bowl, cover and microwave on HIGH for 1½ minutes.
3. Stir the tomato purée, water or stock, aubergine, pasta, tofu and green pepper into the bowl. Push the pasta down so it is covered by the tomato juice. Cover and microwave on HIGH for 9½ minutes.
4. Add the beans, stir well, then microwave on HIGH for 7 minutes, stirring halfway through the cooking time. Leave to stand for 2 minutes.

Selections per serving:
1 Bread
2 Protein
3 Vegetable
25 Optional Calories

PASTA RATATOUILLE

SERVES 3

330 CALORIES PER SERVING

6oz (180g) aubergine

salt

2 teaspoons olive oil

1 onion, chopped

1 large green pepper, seeded and cut into ½-inch (1.25-cm) squares

½ clove garlic, finely chopped

1 tablespoon tomato purée

1 medium (15oz/497g) can chopped tomatoes

9oz (270g) tofu, cut in ½-inch (1.25-cm) cubes

4 tablespoons water or vegetable stock

12oz (360g) mixture drained canned kidney and flageolet beans

3oz (90g) pasta spirals

1. Cut the aubergine into 1-inch (2.5-cm) cubes. Place in a sieve and sprinkle with salt. Leave for 30 minutes to allow the bitter juices to drip out, then rinse well.
2. Heat the oil in a saucepan, add the onion and stir-fry for 2 minutes. Add the green pepper and stir-fry for a further 5 minutes.
3. Stir the garlic, tomato purée, chopped tomatoes, tofu, water or stock, beans and aubergine into the saucepan. Mix all the ingredients well together, bring to the boil, then cover the saucepan, reduce the heat and simmer for 20–25 minutes.
4. While the vegetables are cooking boil a saucepan of water, add the pasta and cook for about 8 minutes until almost but not quite cooked, then drain.
5. Stir the pasta into the simmering vegetables, mix well, cover and simmer for a further 10 minutes.

Selections per serving:
  1 Bread
  ½ Fat
  2 Protein
  3½ Vegetable
  35 Optional Calories

CHICKEN WITH CORN SAUCE

SERVES 2

235 CALORIES PER SERVING

The sauce will not be smooth as a liquidiser won't process the mixture to a smooth purée.

2 × 5oz (150g) skinned chicken breasts

3oz (90g) drained canned sweetcorn

4 tablespoons water

2 tablespoons orange juice

1½ teaspoon cornflour

¾ teaspoon sugar

1½ teaspoons finely chopped spring onions

½ teaspoon chopped tarragon

Tip:
To save money buy 5½oz (165g) chicken breasts and remove the skin yourself.

1. Lay the chicken breasts on a plate and place in a roasting bag. Slit the bag then tuck under the plate. Microwave on HIGH for 5 minutes. Leave to stand while preparing and cooking the sauce.
2. Place the sweetcorn, water and 1 tablespoon orange juice in a liquidiser. Process for a few seconds.
3. Blend the cornflour in a small basin and blend to a smooth paste with the remaining orange juice. Stir in the sweetcorn purée and sugar. Add the spring onions and tarragon.
4. Transfer the basin to the microwave and cook on HIGH for 1 minute. Stir well then cook for a further minute, stirring halfway through.
5. Arrange the chicken breasts on two serving plates and spoon the sauce over.

Selections per serving:
    ½ Bread
    3 Protein
    25 Optional Calories

CONVENTIONAL METHOD

SERVES 2

225 CALORIES PER SERVING

ingredients as above

Selections per serving:
    ½ Bread
    3 Protein
    25 Optional Calories

1. Lay the chicken, skin side down, on the rack of a grill pan. Cook under a moderate grill for 5 minutes, turn and cook for a further 8 minutes.
2. Place the sweetcorn, water and 1 tablespoon orange juice in a liquidiser. Process for a few seconds.
3. Place the cornflour in a small saucepan, and blend to a smooth paste with the remaining orange juice. Stir in the sweetcorn purée and sugar. Add the spring onion and tarragon.
4. Heat the corn sauce over a moderate heat until boiling. Boil for 1 minute, stirring all the time.
5. Remove the skin from the chicken breasts, arrange on serving plates and spoon the corn sauce over.

FENNEL AU GRATIN

SERVES 2

190 CALORIES PER SERVING

Ideal for a quick, light lunch or supper dish.

1 tablespoon cornflour

¼ pint (150ml) skimmed milk

2oz (60g) cheese, finely grated

2 small bulbs fennel – total weight about 11oz (330g)

Tip:
When cooking vegetables in the microwave always season after cooking.

1. Measure the cornflour into a 1 pint (600ml) bowl. Gradually blend in the milk and microwave on HIGH for 2 minutes or until boiling, stirring every 40–45 seconds. Remove from the oven.
2. Reserve about a tablespoon of cheese, add the rest to the sauce and stir until melted.
3. Trim the fennel and reserve any feathery leaves for garnish. Cut the bulbs lengthways into quarters. Place the fennel and 6 tablespoons of water in a container. Cover and microwave on HIGH for 8 minutes. Put to one side.
4. Reheat the cheese sauce on HIGH for 30 seconds and stir well.
5. Drain the fennel, arrange in a serving dish and pour the hot cheese sauce over, then sprinkle with the reserved cheese. Return to the microwave and cook on HIGH for 30–40 seconds until the cheese sauce has melted.

Selections per serving:
   ¼ Milk
   1 Protein
   1½ Vegetable
   15 Optional Calories

FENNEL AU GRATIN

SERVES 4

190 CALORIES PER SERVING

If conventional methods are used to make this recipe it is important to increase the quantities as it would be extremely difficult to make the 1/4 pint (150ml) sauce included in the microwave instructions.

4 small bulbs fennel

salt

2 tablespoons cornflour

1/2 pint (300ml) skimmed milk

4oz (120g) cheese, finely grated

1. Trim the fennel and reserve any feathery leaves for garnish. Cut each bulb of fennel lengthways into quarters.
2. Cook the fennel in boiling salted water for 15–20 minutes, drain and place cut side down in a flameproof dish.
3. While the fennel is cooking make the sauce. Blend the cornflour to a smooth paste with a little milk. Heat the remaining milk in a small saucepan. Stir the steaming milk into the cornflour paste then bring to the boil, stirring all the time. Boil for 1–2 minutes.
4. Reserve about a tablespoon of cheese and stir the remainder into the sauce.
5. Pour the cheese sauce over the bulbs of fennel, sprinkle with the reserved cheese and grill under a high heat until golden and bubbling. Garnish with reserved fennel leaves and serve.

Selections per serving:
1/4 Milk
1 Protein
1 1/2 Vegetable
15 Optional Calories

BLUE CHEESE BEEF

SERVES 4

300 CALORIES PER SERVING

Don't use chopped frozen spinach, it can't be as well-drained as the leaves.

1lb (480g) minced beef

2 tablespoons plus 2 teaspoons cornflour

½ pint (300ml) skimmed milk

1 leek or onion, chopped

1 small (8oz/227g) can chopped tomatoes

½ teaspoon marjoram

2oz (60g) mushrooms, sliced

8oz (240g) frozen leaf spinach

2oz (60g) blue cheese, e.g. Danish blue

Tip:
While the Blue Cheese Beef is standing, cook a green vegetable to accompany it.

1. Form the minced beef into 5 or 6 patties, place on the rack of a grill pan and cook, turning once, until the fat stops dripping.
2. Blend 2 tablespoons of cornflour with the milk. Microwave uncovered on HIGH for 1½ minutes, stir well, then return to the microwave and cook on HIGH for 1 minute.
3. Place the leek or onion in a container with 2 tablespoons of water. Cover and cook on HIGH for 4 minutes.
4. Gradually stir the chopped tomatoes into the remaining cornflour. Drain the leek or onion and stir into the tomatoes. Add the marjoram, mushrooms and crumble in the beef, cover and cook on HIGH for 10 minutes. Stir once during the cooking time. Remove from the oven and leave to stand, covered.
5. Place the spinach and 2 tablespoons of water in a container, cover and cook on HIGH for 6 minutes.
6. Remove the spinach and return the white sauce to the oven. Reheat on HIGH for 1 minute.
7. Drain the spinach. Press the spinach as hard as you can against a sieve to remove as much water as possible.
8. Spread the spinach over the base of a microwave-safe serving dish. Spoon the beef mixture on top. Crumble the cheese into the white sauce, stir well and pour over the beef. Return to the oven and cook on HIGH for 1 minute. Leave to stand for 3–4 minutes.

Selections per serving:
¼ Milk
4 Protein
2 Vegetable
20 Optional Calories

BLUE CHEESE BEEF

SERVES 4

325 CALORIES PER SERVING

1lb (480g) minced beef

2 teaspoons vegetable oil

1 leek or onion, chopped

4 teaspoons plain flour

1 small (8oz/227g) can chopped tomatoes

½ teaspoon marjoram

2oz (60g) mushrooms, sliced

6 tablespoons stock

salt and pepper

8oz (240g) frozen leaf spinach

2 tablespoons cornflour

½ pint (300ml) skimmed milk

2oz (60g) blue cheese e.g. Danish blue

1. Form the minced beef into five or six patties, place on the rack of a grill pan and cook, turning once, until the fat stops dripping.
2. Heat the oil in a saucepan, add the leek or onion and stir-fry for 5 minutes until limp. Add the flour and stir round.
3. Stir the tomatoes, marjoram, mushrooms and stock into the saucepan. Crumble in the beef and season well with salt and pepper. Place the saucepan over a moderate heat and bring to the boil, cover, reduce the heat and leave to simmer for 10 minutes, then simmer for a further 10 minutes uncovered.
4. Cook the spinach according to its packaging instructions then drain very well, squeezing out as much moisture as possible.
5. Mix the cornflour to a smooth paste with a little milk. Heat the remaining milk until steaming, stir in the cornflour paste and bring to the boil, stirring all the time. Boil for 2 minutes.
6. Crumble or grate the cheese and stir into the sauce.
7. Spread the spinach evenly over the base of an ovenproof dish. Spoon the minced beef mixture on top and cover with the cheese sauce. Bake at 400°F, 200°C, Gas Mark 6 for 20 minutes.

Selections per serving:
½ Fat
¼ Milk
4 Protein
2 Vegetable
25 Optional Calories

BAVARIAN PORK

SERVES 4

280 CALORIES PER SERVING

If possible use an uncooked beetroot for this recipe but if they are not available, roughly chop a medium-sized one and add it with the red cabbage etc.

12oz (360g) pork

2 teaspoons margarine

1 large onion

1 tablespoon cornflour

1 tablespoon wine vinegar

8fl oz (240ml) apple juice

1 tablespoon sugar

1 medium raw beetroot, grated

12oz (360g) red cabbage, finely shredded

8 tablespoons soured cream

Tip:
If you prefer, substitute the soured cream with low-fat natural yogurt and deduct 45 Calories from the amount given for each serving.

1. Lay the pork on the rack of a grill pan and grill under a moderate heat, turning once, until the fat stops dripping.
2. Place the margarine in a large bowl and microwave on HIGH for 1 minute. Cut the onion in half then cut each half into thin slices. Add the onion to the basin, cover and microwave on HIGH for 3 minutes.
3. Dice the pork. Blend the cornflour to a smooth paste with the vinegar and a little apple juice. Stir in the remaining apple juice then add the pork and apple juice to the onion.
4. Sprinkle the sugar into the bowl. Add the beetroot and red cabbage and stir well.
5. Cover the basin and cook on HIGH for 5 minutes, stir well, then cook on HIGH for 7 minutes. Leave to stand for 4 minutes.
6. Spoon the Bavarian Pork into four warm bowls or onto four warm plates and spoon the soured cream in the centre.

Selections per serving:
$\frac{1}{2}$ Fat
$\frac{1}{2}$ Fruit
$2\frac{1}{2}$ Protein
$1\frac{1}{4}$ Vegetable
90 Optional Calories

BAVARIAN PORK

SERVES 4

280 CALORIES PER SERVING

12oz (360g) lean pork

1 large onion

2 teaspoons margarine

1 tablespoon cornflour

1 tablespoon wine vinegar

8fl oz (240ml) apple juice

1 tablespoon sugar

1 medium raw beetroot, finely shredded

12oz (360g) red cabbage, finely shredded

8 tablespoons soured cream

1. Place the pork on the rack of a grill pan and cook under a moderate heat, turning once, until the fat stops dripping. Allow to cool a little then dice into small pieces.
2. Cut the onion in half then cut each half into thin slices.
3. Melt the margarine in a saucepan over a moderate heat, add the onion and stir-fry for 4–5 minutes.
4. Blend the cornflour to a smooth paste with the vinegar and apple juice. Stir the cornflour paste, remaining apple juice, sugar, beetroot, red cabbage and pork into the saucepan. Bring to the boil, stirring all the time. Cover, reduce the heat and leave to simmer for 20–30 minutes until the pork and cabbage are cooked.
5. Spoon the Bavarian Pork into four warm bowls or onto four warm plates and spoon the soured cream in the centre.

Selections per serving:
  ½ Fat
  ½ Fruit
  2½ Protein
  1¼ Vegetable
  90 Optional Calories

BANANA AND BREAD PUDDING

SERVES 2

230 CALORIES PER SERVING

If the custard isn't just set, return to the oven for a few seconds on a low setting.

3oz (90g) fruit malt loaf

½ pint (300ml) skimmed milk

I teaspoon honey

I egg, beaten

good pinch of ground allspice

½ medium banana, sliced

Tip:
Brush the cut surface of the banana with lemon juice to use the next day.

1. Cut the bread in very thin slices and then dice into small pieces. If the bread is too sticky pull the slices apart into small pieces.
2. Place the milk and honey in the microwave oven and cook on HIGH for 2 minutes. Pour the steaming milk onto the egg and mix well.
3. Arrange half the bread over the base of a 1½ or 2 pint (900 or 1200ml) dish. Sprinkle with the allspice, cover the bread with the slices of banana and then top with the remaining bread.
4. Strain the milk over the pudding then cover tightly with clingfilm and cook on MEDIUM for 4½ minutes, then LOW for 12 minutes. Leave to stand for 5 minutes, uncover and serve.

Selections per serving:

1½ Bread	½ Protein
½ Fruit	10 Optional Calories
½ Milk	

CONVENTIONAL METHOD

SERVES 2

240 CALORIES PER SERVING

½ teaspoon margarine

3oz (90g) fruit malt loaf

½ pint (300ml) skimmed milk

I teaspoon honey

I egg, beaten

good pinch of ground allspice

½ medium banana, sliced

Selections per serving:

1½ Bread	½ Protein
½ Fruit	20 Optional Calories
½ Milk	

1. Grease a 1½ pint (900ml) ovenproof dish with the margarine.
2. Cut the bread into very thin slices and then dice or, if the bread is sticky, pull into small pieces.
3. Heat the milk and honey in a small saucepan until steaming. Add the hot milk to the egg and mix well.
4. Arrange half the bread evenly over the base of the dish. Sprinkle with the allspice then cover with the banana slices and the remaining bread.
5. Strain the hot milk and egg over the pudding and leave to stand for 20 minutes.
6. Bake at 325°F, 160°C, Gas Mark 3 for 40–45 minutes until just set.

SAVOURY SAUCES

The following recipes are all cornflour-based savoury sauces. The microwave oven enables small quantities of sauce to be made without forming lumps or burning. Infused milk gives sauces a better flavour but if you are short of time, substitute ordinary skimmed milk.

BASIC WHITE SAUCE

SERVES 2

50 CALORIES PER SERVING

¼ pint (150ml) skimmed milk

¼–½ onion

4 whole cloves

I tablespoon cornflour

salt and pepper

Tip:
If the sauces have to be made ahead of time lay a sheet of damp greaseproof paper or clingfilm over the top of the sauce – this will prevent a skin forming.

1. Place the milk, onion and cloves in a bowl and microwave on HIGH for I ½ minutes. Put to one side and leave for 15–20 minutes or until cool.
2. Strain the milk and gradually blend into the cornflour.
3. Place the sauce in the microwave and cook on HIGH for 2½ minutes, stirring well after the first minute then every 20–30 seconds.
4. Remove the boiling sauce from the microwave and season well.

Selections per serving:
¼ Milk
15 Optional Calories

PARSLEY SAUCE (serves 2)   50 Calories per serving – add I tablespoon of chopped parsley to the blended milk, cook as above.

Serve with vegetables, fish or ham.

Selections per serving:
¼ Milk
15 Optional Calories

PRAWN SAUCE (serves 2)   80 Calories per serving – add 2oz (60g) roughly chopped peeled prawns to the blended cornflour and milk, cook as above, adding a little lemon juice after cooking.

Serve with hard-boiled eggs or white fish.

Selections per serving:
¼ Milk
1 Protein
15 Optional Calories

CHEESE SAUCE (serves 2)   135 Calories per serving – add 1½oz (45g) finely grated cheese and ½ teaspoon mustard to the completed sauce.

Serve with hard-boiled eggs, white fish or vegetables.

Selections per serving:
¼ Milk
¾ Protein
15 Optional Calories

MUSHROOM SAUCE (serves 3)   55 Calories per serving – add 4oz (120g) mushrooms, finely chopped, 1 teaspoon cornflour, 1 tablespoon milk. Place the mushrooms in a basin, cover and microwave on HIGH for 2½ minutes. Continue from point 2 in the instructions, add the extra cornflour and milk, then blend together. Stir into the cooked mushrooms and proceed as instructed.

Serve with vegetables, beef, ham or white fish.

Selections per serving:
¼ Milk
½ Vegetable
20 Optional Calories

BAKED POTATOES

SERVES 1

130 CALORIES PER SERVING

Could a microwave section be complete without baked potatoes? The following ideas are suitable for snacks or to serve with main meals.

6oz (180g) potato

Tip:
Alternatively, bake at 350°–400°F, 180°–200°C, Gas Mark 4–6 for 50 minutes to 1 hour 15 minutes.

1. Wash and dry the potato. Pierce the skin in several places and lay on a double thickness of kitchen paper. Microwave on HIGH for 4½ minutes. Wrap in aluminium foil and leave to stand for 3–4 minutes.

Selections per serving:
2 Bread

FILLED POTATOES FOR ONE

285 CALORIES PER SERVING

6oz (180g) potato

1 tablespoon skimmed milk

2 teaspoons tomato ketchup

1 tablespoon chopped spring onions

2oz (60g) corned beef, diced

1. Cook the potato as previously described. Scoop out the middle, leaving the skins as shells.
2. Mash the potato with the milk and ketchup. Stir in the onions and corned beef.
3. Spoon the filling into the skins, place on the kitchen paper and microwave on HIGH for 1½ minutes. Leave to stand for 1 minute.

Selections per serving:
2 Bread
2 Protein
10 Optional Calories

245 CALORIES PER SERVING

6oz (180g) potato

1½oz (45g) frozen mixed vegetables

1 tablespoon skimmed milk

2oz (60g) curd cheese

Selections per serving:
2 Bread
1 Protein
½ Vegetable
5 Optional Calories

1. Cook the potato as previously described and during standing time prepare the filling.
2. Place the vegetables in a suitable container, cover and microwave on HIGH for 1½ minutes.
3. Scoop out the middle of the potato, leaving the skins as shells. Mash the potato with the milk and curd cheese. Drain the vegetables and stir into the mashed potato. Spoon back into the skins, place on the kitchen paper and microwave on HIGH for 1 minute. Leave to stand for 1 minute.

275 CALORIES PER SERVING

6oz (180g) potato

4 teaspoons skimmed milk

2 teaspoons low-calorie mayonnaise

½ teaspoon lemon juice

2oz (60g) well drained canned sardines

1 tablespoon chopped spring onion

1. Cook the potato as previously described. Scoop out the middle, leaving the skins as shells.
2. Mash the potato, milk, mayonnaise and lemon juice together. Add the sardines and spring onions and mash again.
3. Spoon the filling into the potato skins, place on the kitchen paper and microwave on HIGH for 1½ minutes. Leave to stand for 1 minute.

Selections per serving:
2 Bread
1 Fat
2 Protein
5 Optional Calories

280 CALORIES PER SERVING

6oz (180g) potato

4 teaspoons skimmed milk

2 teaspoons horseradish sauce

2oz (60g) smoked mackerel

Tip:
Always leave the potatoes for the full standing time as they retain heat and can cause burns.

1. Cook the potato as previously described. Scoop out the middle, leaving the skins as shells.
2. Mash the potato with the milk and horseradish sauce.
3. Remove any skin from the mackerel and flake, then mix into the potato.
4. Spoon the filling into the potato skins, place on the kitchen paper and microwave on HIGH for 1½ minutes. Leave to stand for 1 minute.

Selections per serving:
2 Bread
2 Protein
40 Optional Calories

LAMB WITH SWEET POTATOES

SERVES 4

340 CALORIES PER SERVING

Use only lean, tender lamb for this recipe otherwise the power levels will be incorrect and result in the meat being very tough.

1lb 2oz (540g) lean boneless lamb
juice of 2 medium oranges
2 large sprigs of mint
1oz (30g) raisins
6oz (180g) sweet potatoes
6 small pickling onions
1 red pepper, seeded
1 tablespoon cornflour
1 teaspoon honey

Tip:
If sweet potatoes are unavailable substitute ordinary potatoes, but cut them in slightly larger cubes.

1. Lay the lamb on the rack of a grill pan and grill under a moderate heat, turning once, until the fat stops dripping.
2. Cut the lamb into large pieces, about 2-inches (5-cm) square. Place the lamb, juice of one orange, mint and raisins in a bowl, cover and microwave on HIGH for 2½ minutes. Put to one side.
3. Cut the sweet potato into large cubes, halve the onions and cut the pepper into ½-inch (1.25-cm) squares.
4. Pour the remaining orange juice into a bowl, add the vegetables, cover and microwave on HIGH for 5 minutes.
5. While the vegetables are cooking blend the cornflour to a smooth paste with the meat juices, add the honey and stir in the lamb and vegetables. Cover and microwave on MEDIUM for 10 minutes. Leave to stand for 5 minutes.

Selections per serving:
½ Bread
¾ Fruit
3½ Protein
½ Vegetable
10 Optional Calories

Lamb with Sweet Potatoes

LAMB WITH SWEET POTATOES

SERVES 4

370 CALORIES PER SERVING

Any lean cut of lamb can be used for this recipe but remember the tougher the cut the longer the cooking time. Stewing lamb will require about 2¹/₂ hours.

1lb 2oz (540g) lean lamb

6 small pickling onions

1 red pepper, seeded

6oz (180g) sweet potatoes

1 tablespoon vegetable oil

1 tablespoon cornflour

juice of 2 medium oranges

4 tablespoons stock

1 teaspoon honey

1oz (30g) raisins

2 large sprigs of mint

1. Lay the lamb on the rack of a grill pan. Cook under a moderate heat, turning once, until the fat stops dripping. Cut the lamb into 2-inch (5-cm) pieces.
2. Cut the onions in half and cut the red pepper into ¹/₂-inch (1.25-cm) squares. Cut the sweet potato into chunks.
3. Heat the oil in a flameproof casserole, add the onion and stir-fry for 4–5 minutes. Add the red pepper and stir-fry for a further 3–4 minutes. Sprinkle the cornflour over the vegetables, stir well, then remove from the heat.
4. Blend the orange juice and stock into the cornflour and vegetables. Add the lamb, sweet potatoes, honey, raisins and mint, stir well, then cover and cook at 325°F, 160°C, Gas Mark 3 for 1¹/₄–2¹/₂ hours depending on the cut of the lamb.

Selections per serving:
¹/₂ Bread
³/₄ Fat
³/₄ Fruit
3¹/₂ Protein
¹/₂ Vegetable
15 Optional Calories

BLACKCURRANT TOFU FLAN

SERVES 8

165 CALORIES PER SERVING

This flan is made with fresh blackcurrants but if they aren't in season, substitute frozen blackcurrants and alter the cooking time as necessary. To make this recipe for a vegetarian, substitute the gelatine for a vegetable-based gelling agent.

8 large digestive biscuits

8 teaspoons margarine

10oz (300g) blackcurrants

2 tablespoons sugar

10oz (300g) drained silken tofu

1½ teaspoons lemon juice

4½ teaspoons gelatine

5fl oz (150ml) low-fat natural yogurt

> **Tip:**
> If you wish to make this flan without the use of a microwave, melt the margarine in a very small saucepan. Pour 2 tablespoons of water in a small basin, sprinkle in the gelatine and stand in a saucepan of simmering water until dissolved.

1. Crush the biscuits to fine crumbs. Place the margarine in a bowl and microwave on HIGH for 50 seconds.
2. Stir the biscuit crumbs and margarine together and press into a 7-inch (17.5-cm) round loose-bottomed cake tin or flan dish.
3. Place the blackcurrants in a dish or bowl, add 2 tablespoons of water, cover and cook on HIGH for 2½ minutes. Stir in the sugar and leave to cool.
4. Spoon the blackcurrants, tofu and lemon juice into a blender or food processor and process until smooth.
5. Pour 2 tablespoons of water in a cup or small basin and cook on HIGH for 30 seconds. Sprinkle the gelatine into the hot water, stir well and leave until dissolved. If necessary microwave for a few seconds to reheat the water.
6. Pour the dissolved gelatine into the blackcurrant purée and process until mixed. Reserve 2 teaspoons of yogurt, place the rest of the yogurt into the purée and process once again, then pour on top of the biscuit base. Spoon the reserved yogurt unevenly over the flan and gently swirl over the flan with a fork.
7. Chill the flan until set. If the flan is in a cake tin, remove and slide onto a flat serving plate.

Selections per serving:
   1 Bread
   1 Fat
   ¼ Fruit
   ¼ Protein
   35 Optional Calories

LAMB WITH DUMPLINGS

SERVES 4

400 CALORIES PER SERVING

Dumplings – what a treat!

1lb 2oz (540g) lean boneless lamb

1 large onion

2 sticks celery

1lb (480g) mixed root vegetables, e.g. swede, turnip, carrot

1 tablespoon cornflour

½ pint (300ml) stock

1 tablespoon tomato purée

2oz (60g) self-raising flour

good pinch of mixed herbs

2 tablespoons margarine

Tip:
If you wish to serve the Lamb with Dumplings directly from the microwave, place the meat and vegetables in a suitable serving dish between points 6 and 7, then proceed as directed.

---

1. Lay the lamb on the rack of a grill pan and grill under a moderate heat, turning once, until the fat stops dripping.
2. Cut the lamb into 1½-inch (4-cm) cubes.
3. Thickly slice the onion and celery. Cut the root vegetables into 1½-inch (4-cm) chunks.
4. Blend the cornflour to a paste with a little stock, then add the remaining stock and tomato purée.
5. Stir the lamb, vegetables and stock into a bowl, cover and microwave on HIGH for 12 minutes, then stir well. Reduce the setting to LOW and cook for 50 minutes.
6. After 45 minutes make the dumplings: sieve the flour into a bowl, stir in the mixed herbs and rub in the margarine (if possible margarine which has been stored in the freezer). Mix with 1–1½ tablespoons of cold water to form a soft dough. Using your hands roll into four balls.
7. Stir the meat and vegetables. Place the dumplings on top, cover and microwave on HIGH for 12 minutes. Leave to stand for 5 minutes.

Selections per serving:
½ Bread
1½ Fat
3½ Protein
2 Vegetable
10 Optional Calories

LAMB WITH DUMPLINGS

SERVES 4

420 CALORIES PER SERVING

Ilb 2oz (540g) lean lamb

I large onion

2 sticks celery

Ilb (480g) mixed root vegetables, e.g. swede, turnip, carrot

2 teaspoons oil

I tablespoon cornflour

14fl oz (420ml) stock

I tablespoon tomato purée

salt and pepper

2oz (60g) self-raising flour

good pinch of mixed herbs

2 tablespoons margarine

1. Lay the lamb on the rack of a grill pan and grill under a moderate heat, turning once, until the fat stops dripping. Cut the lamb into 1½-inch (4-cm) cubes.
2. Thickly slice the onion and celery and cut the root vegetables into 1½-inch (4-cm) chunks.
3. Heat the oil in a flameproof casserole, add the onion and stir-fry for about 4 minutes until limp.
4. Sprinkle the cornflour over the onion, stir round, then remove from the heat and gradually add the stock and tomato purée.
5. Stir the celery, root vegetables and lamb into the casserole, season with salt and pepper, then cover and cook at 325°F, 160°C, Gas Mark 3 for I hour 20 minutes.
6. Twenty minutes before the end of the cooking time make the dumplings: sieve the flour into a bowl and stir in the mixed herbs. Rub in the margarine (if possible margarine which has been stored in the freezer). Mix with 1–1½ tablespoons of cold water to form a soft dough. Using your hands roll the dough into four balls.
7. Stir the meat and vegetables, place the dumplings on top, cover and return to the oven for a further 15–20 minutes.

Selections per serving:
½ Bread
2 Fat
3½ Protein
2 Vegetable
10 Optional Calories

SWEET PORK

SERVES 4

355 CALORIES PER SERVING

Any cut of pork may be used for this recipe but remove all the visible fat before weighing and precooking. Some cuts of pork have a considerable amount of fat.

14oz (420g) pork

1 clove garlic, finely chopped

1 onion, chopped

6oz (180g) drained canned pineapple chunks, 2 tablespoons juice reserved

1 tablespoon lemon juice

1 tablespoon tomato purée

½ teaspoon chilli sauce

1 tablespoon honey

1 teaspoon Worcestershire sauce

1 tablespoon cornflour

6fl oz (180ml) stock or water

12oz (360g) sweet potatoes, or potatoes cut in chunks

Tip:
To measure honey accurately, lightly grease the measuring spoon, it will run easily off the spoon.

1. Lay the pork on the rack of a grill pan and grill under a moderate heat, turning once, until the fat stops dripping. Cut the pork into 1½-inch (4-cm) cubes.
2. Place the garlic, onion, pineapple juice, lemon juice, tomato purée, chilli sauce, honey and Worcestershire sauce in a bowl or microwave casserole dish.
3. Blend the cornflour and stock together and stir into the pineapple juice etc. Cover and microwave on HIGH for 5 minutes.
4. Stir the pineapple into the sauce, mix well, then add the pork and stir once again, cover and cook on HIGH for 3 minutes.
5. Stir the sweet potatoes into the pork stew, cover and cook on HIGH for 9 minutes. Stir once or twice during cooking. Leave to stand for 3–4 minutes.

Selections per serving:
 1 Bread
 ¼ Fruit
 3 Protein
 ¼ Vegetable
 35 Optional Calories

SWEET PORK

SERVES 4

375 CALORIES PER SERVING

14oz (420g) lean pork

2 teaspoons oil

1 clove garlic, finely chopped

1 onion, chopped

6oz (180g) drained canned pineapple chunks, 2 tablespoons juice reserved

1 tablespoon cornflour

1 tablespoon lemon juice

1 tablespoon tomato purée

½ teaspoon chilli sauce

1 tablespoon honey

1 teaspoon Worcestershire sauce

6fl oz (180ml) stock

12oz (360g) sweet potatoes or potatoes, cut in chunks

salt and pepper

1. Lay the pork on the rack of a grill pan, grill under a moderate heat and cook, turning once, until the fat stops dripping. Cut the pork into 1½-inch (4-cm) cubes.
2. Heat the oil in a flameproof casserole, add the garlic and onion and stir-fry for 4–5 minutes until the onion is translucent.
3. Blend the pineapple juice and cornflour together, pour into the hot onion and stir well. Add the pineapple chunks, lemon juice, tomato purée, chilli sauce, honey, Worcestershire sauce and stock.
4. Cut the sweet potatoes into chunks. Stir the pork and sweet potatoes into the sweet sauce, season with salt and pepper and bake at 350°F, 180°C, Gas Mark 4 for 1¼–1½ hours.

Selections per serving:
1 Bread
½ Fat
¼ Fruit
3 Protein
¼ Vegetable
35 Optional Calories

SCRAMBLED EGGS

The following basic recipe and variations may be served with toast as a snack meal for two people. However, if you prefer, serve the whole recipe as a main meal for one and double the Selections and calories.

BASIC RECIPE

SERVES 2

115 CALORIES PER SERVING

1 teaspoon margarine

2 eggs

4 tablespoons skimmed milk

salt and pepper

Tip:
Always remove scrambled eggs from the microwave when semi-set. The standing time should complete the cooking but if necessary return to the oven for a few seconds. They should have a creamy, not dry, texture.

1. Place the margarine in a bowl and microwave on HIGH for 30 seconds.
2. Beat the eggs and milk together, pour into the melted margarine and microwave on HIGH for 50 seconds. Stir well from the outside of the bowl towards the centre.
3. Return to the oven and microwave on HIGH for a further 1–1¼ minutes, stirring every 20 seconds.
4. Cover and leave to stand for 1 minute. Season with a little salt and pepper and serve.

Selections per serving:
½ Fat
1 Protein
10 Optional Calories

CHEESEY SCRAMBLE   200 Calories per serving – add 1½oz (45g) finely grated cheese to the eggs and milk and cook as above allowing a little extra cooking time.

Selections per serving:
½ Fat
1¾ Protein
10 Optional Calories

MUSHROOM SCRAMBLE   120 Calories per serving – place 2oz (60g) chopped mushrooms with the margarine in a bowl, cover and microwave on HIGH for 1½ minutes, then proceed as above.

Selections per serving:
½ Fat
1 Protein
¼ Vegetable
10 Optional Calories

Scrambled Eggs

PEAR AND GINGER CRUMBLE

SERVES 4

265 CALORIES PER SERVING

This crumble is topped with an oatmeal mixture but, if you prefer, you can substitute flour.

1lb 4oz (600g) pears, peeled, quartered and cored

1½–2½ teaspoons finely chopped ginger

2 teaspoons granulated or caster sugar

4oz (120g) fine or medium oatmeal

8 teaspoons margarine

1 tablespoon demerara sugar

Tip:
White flour results in an anaemic topping whereas wholemeal flour gives a more traditional appearance.

1. Mix the pears, ginger and white sugar together, then transfer to a deep dish 6–7 inches (15–17.5cm) in diameter. Add 4 tablespoons of water.
2. Spoon the oatmeal into a bowl and add the margarine (if possible margarine which has been stored in the freezer). Rub the margarine into the oatmeal until the mixture resembles fine breadcrumbs.
3. Stir 2 teaspoons of demerara sugar into the oatmeal topping, then spoon over the fruit. Level the top then sprinkle with the remaining demerara sugar.
4. Place the crumble, uncovered, in the microwave and cook on HIGH for 12 minutes. Leave to stand for 3–4 minutes.

Selections per serving:
  1 Bread
  2 Fat
  1¼ Fruit
  25 Optional Calories

CONVENTIONAL METHOD

PEAR AND GINGER CRUMBLE

SERVES 4

265 CALORIES PER SERVING

If the pears are very large, such as Comice, either slice thickly or cut each one into eight pieces.

1lb 4oz (600g) pears, peeled, quartered and cored

1½–2½ teaspoons finely chopped ginger

5 teaspoons sugar

4oz (120g) fine or medium oatmeal

8 teaspoons margarine

1. Place the pears in a medium-sized saucepan, add the ginger and 4–6 tablespoons of water – there must be sufficient liquid to cook the pears without burning. Cover the saucepan and place over a low to moderate heat for 10–15 minutes or until the pears are half cooked.
2. Transfer the pears to a deep 6–7-inch (15–17.5-cm) diameter ovenproof dish. Stir 2 teaspoons of sugar into their cooking liquid and pour over the fruit.
3. Spoon the oatmeal into a bowl and add the margarine (if possible margarine which has been stored in the freezer). Rub the margarine into the oatmeal until the mixture resembles fresh breadcrumbs.
4. Stir the remaining sugar into the oatmeal and sprinkle evenly over the fruit.
5. Bake at 400°F, 200°C, Gas Mark 6 for 20 minutes.

Selections per serving:
   1 Bread
   2 Fat
   1¼ Fruit
   25 Optional Calories

FRUIT SPONGE PUDDING

SERVES 6

210 CALORIES PER SERVING

This microwaved pudding saves a considerable amount of time when compared with a similar conventional pudding.

3 tablespoons margarine

3 tablespoons caster sugar

1½ teaspoons golden syrup

1 egg, beaten

4oz (120g) self-raising flour

good pinch of cinnamon

1 medium dessert apple, peeled, quartered, cored and grated

2oz (60g) sultanas

2½ tablespoons water

> **Tip:**
> Adding a little golden syrup to the pudding prevents it from drying.

1. Grease a 1½ pint (900ml) pudding basin with a little of the margarine.
2. Cream the remaining margarine, caster sugar and golden syrup together. Gradually beat in about half of the egg.
3. Sieve the flour and cinnamon and spoon 2 tablespoons into the creamed mixture. Beat in the remaining egg.
4. Stir in the apple and sultanas then fold in the remaining flour and water.
5. Spoon the mixture into the greased basin and cover with a pleated sheet of clingfilm. Pull the clingfilm up in the centre and prick two or three times with a fork.
6. Microwave the pudding on MEDIUM for 1½ minutes, then on HIGH for 4 minutes. Leave to stand for 4–5 minutes then turn out onto a serving plate.

Selections per serving:
½ Bread
1½ Fat
½ Fruit
60 Optional Calories

Fruit Sponge Pudding and Chocolate Cake

FRUIT SPONGE PUDDING

SERVES 6

200 CALORIES PER SERVING

The grated apple gives this pudding a lovely moist texture. If using an aluminium saucepan for steaming add a little vinegar or lemon juice to prevent the water marking the pan.

3 tablespoons margarine

3 tablespoons caster sugar

1 egg, beaten

4oz (120g) self-raising flour

good pinch of cinnamon

1 medium dessert apple, peeled, quartered, cored and grated

2oz (60g) sultanas

1. Grease a 1½ pint (900ml) pudding basin with a little of the margarine.
2. Cream the remaining margarine and caster sugar together until light and fluffy, then gradually beat in about half the egg.
3. Sieve the flour and cinnamon and spoon 2 tablespoons into the creamed mixture. Beat in the remaining egg.
4. Stir in the apple and sultanas then fold in the flour.
5. Spoon the mixture into the greased basin and cover with a pleated sheet of greaseproof paper. Tie the paper in place with string and place on a plate or saucer lying on the base of a saucepan about a quarter full of simmering water. Cover the saucepan and steam the pudding for 1 hour. Check the water hasn't evaporated during cooking and, if necessary, add more boiling water.
6. Carefully lift the pudding from the saucepan, remove the greaseproof paper and turn out onto a serving plate.

Selections per serving:
½ Bread
1½ Fat
½ Fruit
55 Optional Calories

APRICOT CHEESECAKE

SERVES 6

260 CALORIES PER SERVING

Use a deep, loose-bottomed flan tin for this recipe. The sides should be at least 1½ inches (4.5cm) high, or the filling will spill over the edge – this recipe gives really generous portions! To make this recipe for a vegetarian, substitute the gelatine for a vegetable-based gelling agent.

For the base:

6 large digestive biscuits

3 tablespoons margarine

For the topping:

10 medium apricots

juice of ½ a lemon

6oz (180g) curd cheese

6 tablespoons caster sugar

2 tablespoons hot water

1 sachet gelatine

few drops of almond essence

2 egg whites

pinch of cream of tartar

For the decoration:

1 medium apricot

½ teaspoon lemon juice

2½oz (75g) raspberries

Tip:
If you wish to make this flan without the use of a microwave, place the margarine in a small saucepan and heat gently until melted. Pour 2 tablespoons of hot water in a small basin, sprinkle in the gelatine and stand in a saucepan of simmering water until dissolved.

1. Place the biscuits in a plastic bag and crush with a rolling pin to make fine crumbs. Place the margarine in a bowl and microwave on HIGH for 50 seconds until melted, stir in the biscuit crumbs. Mix well, then press into a serving flan dish or loose-bottomed 7½-inch (19-cm) flan tin.
2. Plunge 10 apricots in boiling water and leave for 1 minute. Drain and place in cold water. Remove the skin from each apricot, halve and discard the stones. Transfer the apricot halves and lemon juice to a blender and process until smooth.
3. Beat together the curd cheese and caster sugar; mix in the apricot purée.
4. Measure the water into a small bowl, microwave on HIGH for 40 seconds, sprinkle in the gelatine, stir well and leave until dissolved. If necessary reheat for a few seconds.
5. Stir the dissolved gelatine and a few drops of almond essence into the cheese and apricot purée. Leave until beginning to set.
6. Whisk the egg whites and cream of tartar until peaking. Using a metal spoon, fold the egg whites evenly into the cheese and apricot mixture. Spoon the mixture onto the biscuit base and chill until completely set.
7. To serve: halve the apricot, remove the stone and cut the fruit into thin wedges. Brush each wedge with lemon juice. If the cheesecake is in a loose-bottomed tin, carefully remove by sliding a spatula or palette knife under the biscuit base and sliding the cheesecake onto a plate. Decorate with the apricot wedges and raspberries.

Selections per serving:
  1 Bread
  1½ Fat
  1 Fruit
  ½ Protein
  65 Optional Calories

CHOCOLATE CAKE

SERVES 12

175 CALORIES PER SERVING

Cakes cooked in a microwave tend to dry out much quicker than cakes baked in a conventional oven. By adding a little golden syrup to the mixture it is possible to moisten the cake a little, but it won't keep as well as conventionally cooked mixtures.

6 tablespoons margarine

6 tablespoons caster sugar

1 teaspoon golden syrup

2 large eggs, beaten

2 tablespoons cocoa

6oz (180g) self-raising flour

¼ teaspoon baking powder

few drops of vanilla essence

3 tablespoons water

4 tablespoons black cherry jam

¼ teaspoon icing sugar

Tip:
Line containers for cooking cake mixtures with clingfilm; greased containers produce a moister edge suitable for puddings.

1. Line a 7-inch (17.5-cm) straight-sided dish with clingfilm (I find a soufflé dish is ideal). Smooth out the clingfilm so there are as few wrinkles as possible.
2. Beat the margarine, sugar and golden syrup together. Gradually beat in about half the eggs.
3. Sieve the cocoa, flour and baking powder and fold into the creamed mixture with the remaining eggs, vanilla essence and water.
4. Spoon the cake mixture into the prepared dish and microwave on MEDIUM for 5½ minutes then HIGH for 1 minute. Leave to stand for 4–5 minutes then remove the cake, peel off the clingfilm and place on a cooling rack.
5. When cold cut the cake horizontally in half then sandwich together with the jam. Sprinkle the icing sugar through a fine sieve over the cake.

Selections per serving:
½ Bread
1½ Fat
65 Optional Calories

CHOCOLATE CAKE

SERVES 12

175 CALORIES PER SERVING

To make sure the two layers of the cake rise to the same height, place alternate spoonfuls of mixture in each tin.

6 tablespoons plus ¾ teaspoon margarine

6 tablespoons caster sugar

2 large eggs, beaten

few drops of vanilla essence

2 tablespoons cocoa

6oz (180g) self-raising flour, sieved

3 tablespoons water

4 tablespoons black cherry jam

¼ teaspoon icing sugar

1. Grease the sides of two 7-inch (17.5-cm) sandwich tins with ¾ teaspoon margarine. Line each base with non-stick baking parchment.
2. Beat the remaining margarine and caster sugar together until light and fluffy, then gradually beat in half the eggs and all the vanilla essence.
3. Sieve the cocoa into the beaten mixture and gradually add almost all the remaining egg.
4. Fold in the last of the egg with the flour and water. Spoon into the prepared tins, level the surface and bake at 350°F, 180°C, Gas Mark 4 for about 25 minutes until risen. Turn out onto a wire rack, remove the non-stick baking parchment and leave to cool.
5. Spread one cake with the jam then place the other cake on top and sprinkle the icing sugar through a fine sieve over the top.

Selections per serving:
½ Bread
1½ Fat
65 Optional Calories

ICE CREAM SAUCES

A microwave oven is ideal for making small quantities of rich sweet sauces. As these sauces are high in sugar and fat, follow the cooking times carefully and if in doubt cook for a shorter time, then add extra seconds as necessary.

CHOCOLATE NUT SAUCE

SERVES 4

55 CALORIES PER SERVING

This makes a thick sauce which can be served warm or cold. If it is to be served cold, stir well then spoon onto the ice cream.

¾oz (20g) plain chocolate

1 tablespoon peanut butter

2 tablespoons skimmed milk

1. Break the chocolate into tiny pieces, place in a bowl with the peanut butter. Microwave on HIGH for 1 minute 40 seconds. Stir well, add 1 tablespoon milk and cook on HIGH for 40 seconds.
2. Remove the sauce from the oven, stir well until smooth, then gradually mix in the remaining milk. Serve warm or cold.

Selections per serving:
55 Optional Calories

RICH MOCHA SAUCE

SERVES 4

75 CALORIES PER SERVING

This sauce gives a good-sized serving for ice-creams and speciality sundaes.

2oz (60g) white chocolate

3 tablespoons skimmed milk

1½ teaspoons instant coffee powder

1. Break the chocolate into tiny pieces, place in a bowl and microwave on HIGH for 2½ minutes. Stir well. Mix 2 tablespoons of milk into the chocolate, stir in the coffee and microwave on HIGH for 40 seconds.
2. Remove the sauce from the microwave and stir in the remaining milk – don't worry if one or two grains of coffee remain. Chill. When ready to use, stir well then spoon over the ice cream.

Selections per serving:
75 Optional Calories

Tip:
These sauces may be used to accompany other desserts, such as fresh or baked bananas.

COOKING
FOR ONE

Many people put on weight because 'cooking for one' seems too much bother, and so they end up constantly nibbling snacks or eating take-aways and confectionery.

Cooking for a single person is often not considered a worthwhile topic for a standard cook book, but this section is devoted to simple nutritious meals for one. Many books contain recipes for families or large numbers which cannot easily be reduced, but the majority of the recipes in this chapter have the added advantage that they can be multiplied to serve two, three or more.

Most of these recipes are cooked on the hob or under the grill as this is more economical than heating an oven to cook one dish for one person. However, when a recipe such as Beef Stew (page 173) is cooked in the oven it can be followed by Double Dessert (page 189) which requires the same oven temperature.

If you live on your own or need to cook single portions, ingredients and equipment can present difficulties. Although supermarkets have introduced many self-service departments which are ideal for purchasing small quantities of fruits and vegetables, and some have wet fish counters, they still persist in selling the more economical cuts of meat in family-sized packs. If possible use a butcher or fishmonger where you will receive personal advice, be able to buy the weight you require and have the meat or fish prepared to suit your needs.

Equipment needn't be a problem if you look round cookshops and department stores. Small saucepans and divided saucepans are invaluable; small quantities of sauce evaporate and burn very easily if made in a large pan and a dual or divided saucepan is useful for cooking two vegetables simultaneously over one burner. Small ovens or grill compartments which double as a second oven are useful and economical. A microwave can prove to be an asset for one person and some ideas are included in Chapter Five, Cooking with a Microwave. Similarly the recipes in Chapter Four, Cooking for the Freezer, can frequently be frozen in single portions and then reheated when required.

I hope the following recipes prove that single portion cooking can result in tasty, varied meals which are easy to prepare yet suitable for the weight-conscious.

All recipes marked * are suitable for vegetarians as well as non-vegetarians

STUFFED AUBERGINE

SERVES 1

320 CALORIES PER SERVING

It's worth looking out for small aubergines as they are ideal for one person. This recipe is a delicious way of serving them and it is very easy to do.

6–7oz (180–210g) aubergine

salt

1½ teaspoons olive oil

1 onion, sliced

1 tomato

1½oz (45g) cheese, grated

Tip:
Degorge overgrown courgettes by the same method to remove their bitter juices.

1. Cut the aubergine in half lengthways. Using a grapefruit knife scoop out the inside of the aubergine, leaving about ½ inch (1.25cm) attached to the skin.
2. Sprinkle the inside of each aubergine half liberally with salt and place skin side uppermost in a sieve or colander. Sprinkle the pieces that have been removed from each half with salt and add to the sieve or colander. Leave for 30–40 minutes to allow the bitter juices to drip out.
3. Rinse all of the aubergine thoroughly under cold running water.
4. Boil a saucepan of water, add the aubergine halves and boil for 3 minutes. Drain the halves upside down.
5. While the aubergine halves are cooking chop the scooped-out aubergine. Heat the oil in a heavy-based saucepan and stir-fry the onion for about 5 minutes until limp.
6. Cover the tomato with boiling water, leave for 30–40 seconds then drain and slip its skin off. Chop the tomato.
7. Add the chopped aubergine and tomato to the onion and stir over a moderate heat for about 3 minutes until the moisture from the tomato has evaporated.
8. Remove the tomato and onion mixture from the heat and stir in about 1oz (30g) cheese. Stir round until the cheese has melted then spoon into the aubergine halves, sprinkle with the reserved cheese and place under a hot grill until the cheese is bubbling.

Selections per serving:
 1½ Fat
 1½ Protein
 3 Vegetable

 VEGETARIAN

STUFFED CABBAGE LEAVES

SERVES 1

405 CALORIES PER SERVING

To make this into a more substantial recipe add 1oz (30g) crumbled or grated blue-veined cheese to the rice stuffing and add 1 Protein Selection and 110 Calories to the given amount.

1½oz (45g) long-grain rice

salt

3 large or 6 small cabbage leaves

1 teaspoon oil

½ onion, finely chopped

1oz (30g) raisins or sultanas

½oz (15g) pine nuts

1 small (8oz/227g) can chopped tomatoes

Tip:
Savoy cabbages are ideal for this recipe; they look pretty and retain some of their texture.

1. Cook the rice in boiling salted water according to the packaging instructions until all the water has been absorbed and the rice is fluffy and separate.
2. Plunge the cabbage leaves in a saucepan of boiling water, bring back to the boil and cook for 3 minutes, drain and leave to cool.
3. Cut away the hard base of the central vein of each cabbage leaf.
4. Heat the oil in a small saucepan, add the onion and stir-fry for about 3 minutes until translucent. Remove from the heat and add the rice, raisins and pine nuts.
5. Lay each cabbage leaf flat – if the leaves are small overlap two of them – place a third of the rice stuffing onto each leaf, fold the sides of the leaves over the stuffing then roll into a small parcel.
6. Transfer the cabbage parcels to a medium-sized saucepan, pour over the chopped tomatoes and lay a saucer or small plate on top to help the leaves retain their shape. Place over a low to moderate heat, cover the saucepan and simmer for 15 minutes.
7. Remove the Stuffed Cabbage Leaves from the saucepan with a slotted spoon and increase the heat to boil the tomatoes rapidly and reduce the liquid. Spoon the tomatoes round the cabbage parcels.

Selections per serving:
1½ Bread
1½ Fat
1 Fruit
1 Protein
4 Vegetable

CARROT AND CORIANDER SOUP

SERVES 1

105 CALORIES PER SERVING

This soup can be made quickly while preparing a meal and then cooled and stored in the refrigerator for the following day.

1 teaspoon margarine

½ onion, chopped

4oz (120g) carrots, sliced

2 teaspoons chopped coriander

1–2-inch (2.5–5-cm) strip of orange zest

¼ pint (150ml) stock

salt and pepper

4 tablespoons skimmed milk

lemon juice

Tip:
Use the basic quantities to make a variety of soups: 4oz (120g) swede or parsnip in ¼ pint (150ml) stock.

1. Heat the margarine in a saucepan, add the onion and stir-fry for 2–3 minutes.
2. Stir the carrots, coriander, orange zest and stock into the saucepan. Bring to the boil, season with salt and pepper and cover. Leave over a very low heat for 30 minutes.
3. Remove the orange zest from the saucepan, pour the stock and vegetables into a liquidiser and process to a purée.
4. Pour the carrot purée back into the saucepan, stir in the milk and reheat. Add more salt and pepper and then lemon juice to taste.

Selections per serving:
 1 Fat
 2 Vegetable
 20 Optional Calories

THICK FRANKFURTER SOUP

SERVES 1

280 CALORIES PER SERVING

This soup makes good use of the small quantities left over from other meals. Use one of the small sticks of celery from the heart.

1 teaspoon margarine

1 pickling onion, finely chopped

1 small stick celery plus leaves, finely chopped

1 small carrot, finely chopped

3 or 4 Brussels sprouts, shredded

2 teaspoons tomato purée

7fl oz (210ml) stock

pepper sauce

salt

2oz (60g) frankfurter, sliced

1 tablespoon finely grated Parmesan cheese

Tip:
If you prefer, substitute the Brussels sprouts with a few leaves of shredded cabbage and the frankfurter with knockwurst.

1. Melt the margarine in a saucepan, add the onion and stir-fry for 1–2 minutes.
2. Stir the celery, carrot and Brussels sprouts into the saucepan. Mix the tomato purée and stock together, pour on top of the vegetables, add a dash of pepper sauce and a little salt. Bring to the boil, cover and simmer for 10 minutes.
3. Add the frankfurter to the soup, stir well, then cover and allow to simmer for 15 minutes. Adjust the seasoning, adding a little more pepper sauce.
4. Ladle the thick soup into a warm bowl and sprinkle with the Parmesan cheese.

Selections per serving:
1 Fat
2 Protein
2 Vegetable
45 Optional Calories

BEEF STEW

SERVES 1

240 CALORIES PER SERVING

This stew is cooked for a long time at a low temperature so the meat is tender and the gravy full of flavour. As the oven is on for such a long time make use of it to cook a pudding such as Double Dessert (page 189) at the same time.

4oz (120g) lean stewing steak

½ onion

6oz (180g) mixture of root vegetables, e.g. carrot, celeriac, swede

1 tablespoon flour

4fl oz (120ml) stock

1 tomato, quartered

good pinch of mixed herbs

salt and pepper

1. Lay the stewing steak on the rack of a grill pan and grill, turning once until the fat stops dripping.
2. Chop the onion, cut the root vegetables into 1-inch (2.5-cm) chunks.
3. Cut the steak into five pieces and place in a small ovenproof casserole dish. Sprinkle in the flour and stir round.
4. Gradually mix the stock into the casserole dish and add the prepared vegetables, tomato and herbs. Season well with salt and pepper.
5. Cover the dish and bake at 325°F, 160°C, Gas Mark 3 for 2½–2¾ hours, stirring twice during cooking.

Selections per serving:
  3 Protein
  3 Vegetable
  35 Optional Calories

Tip:
Bake a potato in the oven at the same time to make a complete meal.

CREAMY PORK

SERVES 1

330 CALORIES PER SERVING

Use a heavy-based saucepan for this recipe – it will help prevent the vegetables from burning.

4oz (120g) pork

1 small or 4 pickling onions

1 small courgette

1½oz (45g) small button mushrooms

1½ teaspoons oil

4 tablespoon stock

2 tablespoons soured cream

2 tablespoons low-fat natural yogurt

Tip:
The same quantity of single cream and a little lemon juice may be used in place of the soured cream.

1. Lay the pork on the rack of a grill pan and grill, turning once, until the fat has stopped dripping. Allow to cool then cut into thin strips.
2. Roughly chop the small onion or quarter the pickling onions. Cut the courgette into 1½-inch (4-cm) lengths. Leave the very small mushrooms whole, cut any others in half.
3. Measure the oil into a saucepan and place over a moderate heat. Add the onion and stir-fry for 2 minutes to brown, then reduce the heat and stir-fry for 2–3 minutes until translucent.
4. Stir the pork, courgette, mushrooms and stock into the saucepan. Cover and leave to simmer for about 10–12 minutes until the pork is thoroughly cooked.
5. Remove the saucepan from the heat, stir in the soured cream and yogurt and serve.

Selections per serving:
   1½ Fat
   3 Protein
   2 Vegetable
   90 Optional Calories

CURRIED CHICKEN NOODLES

SERVES 1

460 CALORIES PER SERVING

This filling meal can be made in about 15 minutes. The fine rice vermicelli noodles don't require cooking; just soak in warm water for about 10 minutes. They are now sold in many supermarkets as well as delicatessens and healthfood shops.

2oz (60g) rice noodles

¼–½ red pepper

½ courgette

3–4 spring onions

¼-inch (5-mm) ginger

½ clove garlic

3oz (90g) cooked chicken or turkey

1oz (30g) drained canned pineapple plus 1 tablespoon juice, reserved

2 teaspoons oil

½ teaspoon hot Madras curry powder

1–2 tablespoons soy sauce

Tip:
Transfer the remaining pineapple and juice to a container, cover and store in the refrigerator for up to 2 days.

1. Wash the rice noodles, place in a bowl and completely cover with warm water. Leave for about 10 minutes while preparing the vegetables.
2. Cut the red pepper and courgette into very thin strips, 1–1½-inches (2.5–4-cm) long. Cut the spring onion into ½-inch (1.25-cm) slices.
3. Finely chop the ginger and garlic and cut the cooked chicken in strips. Chop the pineapple.
4. Heat the oil in a saucepan or frying pan. Add the garlic and ginger and stir-fry for 1 minute. Add the curry powder and vegetables and stir-fry for 3 minutes.
5. Drain the noodles and mix the reserved pineapple juice with 1 tablespoon of soy sauce. Add the chicken, pineapple, rice noodles, soy and pineapple sauce to the vegetable mixture and stir-fry over a moderate heat for 2–3 minutes until heated through.
6. Spoon the noodles onto a warm serving plate and sprinkle a little more soy sauce over.

Selections per serving:
  2 Bread
  2 Fat
  ¼ Fruit
  3 Protein

VEGETABLE CURRY

SERVES 1

415 CALORIES PER SERVING

Simmer the curry gently so the vegetables retain their shape yet absorb the flavour.

4oz (120g) aubergine

salt

3oz (90g) potato

1 carrot

1 small onion

3oz (90g) tofu

1 teaspoon oil

1½–2½ teaspoons hot Madras curry powder

2oz (60g) shelled fresh or frozen peas

1oz (30g) split red lentils

½ medium apple, peeled, cored and chopped

½oz (15g) sultanas

2 teaspoons tomato purée

½ pint (300ml) water or vegetable stock

1. Cut the aubergine in chunks, sprinkle with salt and leave in a colander or sieve for 30–40 minutes for the bitter juices to drip away. Rinse well under running cold water.
2. Cut the potato and carrot into ¾-inch (2-cm) pieces. Chop the onion and coarsely grate the tofu.
3. Heat the oil in a saucepan, add the onion and stir-fry for 2–3 minutes.
4. Stir the curry powder into the saucepan then add all the remaining ingredients.
5. Bring to the boil over a moderate heat, stir well, reduce the heat, cover and simmer for 30 minutes. Stir round about every 10 minutes and add a little extra stock or water if necessary.

Selections per serving:
  1 Bread
  1 Fat
  1 Fruit
  2 Protein
  4 Vegetable
  20 Optional Calories

Tip:
Chop the remaining apple and mix with the segments from one tangerine or satsuma and two chopped fresh or dried dates.

RICE PANCAKES

SERVES 1

395 CALORIES PER SERVING

This recipe can be made with cooked rice left over from a previous meal.

½oz (15g) lean rasher smoked back bacon, rind removed

1½oz (45g) long-grain rice, cooked

½oz (15g) mature Cheddar or Parmesan cheese, finely grated

1 egg

salt and pepper

1½ teaspoons oil

Tip:
To prevent the Rice Pancakes sticking, prove the frying pan: heat a small amount of salt in the pan, tip out, wipe round with a sheet of kitchen paper, then add the oil.

---

1. Place the bacon on the rack of a grill pan and cook under a moderate heat, turning once. Chop into small pieces.
2. Mix the bacon, rice and cheese together.
3. Lightly beat the egg, mix into the rice mixture and season well with salt and pepper.
4. Heat 1 teaspoon of oil in a frying pan, tipping the pan so it evenly coats the base. Using a tablespoon, spoon half the rice mixture into the pan and flatten until about ½-inch (1.25-cm) thick.
5. Cook the Rice Pancake over a moderate heat for about 3 minutes until the underside is a deep golden colour and the top is setting. Carefully turn with a fish slice and cook the other side. Keep warm while cooking the remaining mixture. Add the remaining oil to the pan, tilt and proceed as for the first Rice Pancake.

Selections per serving:
  1½ Bread
  1½ Fat
  2½ Protein

BRAISED LAMB CUTLETS

SERVES 1

270 CALORIES PER SERVING

There is no precooking of the lamb as the fat is skimmed off when cooked.

I small leek

4oz (120g) swede, carrot or a mixture of both

I teaspoon oil

2 sprigs of mint

5 tablespoons stock

2 teaspoons tomato purée

7oz (210g) lamb cutlets

salt and pepper

> **Tip:**
> Always weigh the trimmed cutlets to calculate the approximate amount of meat on each one.

1. Before starting to prepare the vegetables place a bowl of cold water in the refrigerator – this will be important to cool the stock quickly and skim off the fat.
2. Cut the leek into ½-inch (1.25-cm) slices. Cut the swede and carrot into 1½-inch (4-cm) sticks.
3. Heat the oil in a saucepan, add the leek and stir-fry for 2–3 minutes.
4. Add the swede, carrot and mint to the saucepan. Stir the stock and tomato purée together and add to the vegetables.
5. Lay the lamb cutlets on top of the vegetables, season with salt and pepper, cover tightly and place over a very low heat for 30 minutes.
6. Using a slotted spoon transfer the lamb and vegetables to a serving plate and keep warm.
7. Strain the stock into a small basin and stand it in a bowl of chilled water – if possible add a few ice cubes to the chilled water.
8. As soon as the fat solidifies on the top of the stock skim it off. Return the stock to the saucepan and bring to the boil, then pour over the lamb and vegetables.

Selections per serving:
I Fat
3½ Protein
2 Vegetable
10 Optional Calories

SIMPLE CHICKEN SALAD

SERVES 1

225 CALORIES PER SERVING

What can you do with cold chicken? After cooking a whole chicken or turkey for guests there is usually a lot of meat over and this recipe makes a delightful change from just cold meat and salad.

2½ tablespoons low-fat natural yogurt

1 tablespoon mango chutney

1 medium apricot, fresh or canned

½oz (15g) sultanas or raisins

good pinch of allspice

squeeze of lemon juice

3oz (90g) cooked chicken, roughly chopped

a few salad leaves

2-inch (5-cm) wedge of cucumber

1 teaspoon chopped chives

Tip:
If you are unable to buy fresh apricots and don't wish to open a can, substitute with ½ a medium dessert apple.

1. Mix the yogurt and mango chutney together in a small bowl. If there are any large pieces of fruit in the chutney cut them into small dice.
2. Cut the fresh apricot in half, remove the stone and chop the fresh or canned fruit into small pieces.
3. Mix the apricot and sultanas into the yogurt and season well with a good pinch of allspice and squeeze of lemon. Stir in the chicken.
4. Shred the salad leaves and cut the cucumber into thin slices. Arrange the leaves and cucumber in a bowl or on a plate.
5. Spoon the chicken and yogurt onto the leaves and sprinkle with the chopped chives.

Selections per serving:
   1 Fruit
   ¼ Milk
   3 Protein
   ½ Vegetable
   50 Optional Calories

SMOKY BEAN SALAD

SERVES 1

360 CALORIES PER SERVING

This salad can be packed in a plastic box and taken to work or eaten as a picnic lunch.

6oz (180g) hot cooked kidney beans

2 teaspoons olive oil

2 teaspoons wine vinegar

good pinch of mustard powder

1 teaspoon chilli sauce

salt

1 tablespoon finely chopped onion

3oz (90g) smoked tofu

1oz (30g) lean rasher smoked back bacon, rind removed

Tip:
Instead of cooking such a small quantity of beans, heat 6oz (180g) canned beans in their liquid or cook double the quantity and incorporate in another recipe such as Parsnip-Topped Pie (page 182).

1. Place the hot beans in a bowl. Spoon the oil, vinegar, mustard, chilli sauce and a little salt into a screw-top jar, secure and shake well to mix. Alternatively whisk together in a small bowl. Pour the dressing over the beans, add the onion and stir, then leave to cool.
2. Cut the tofu into ½-inch (1.25-cm) cubes.
3. Lay the bacon on the rack of a grill pan and cook, turning once, under a moderate grill. Cut into thin strips across the width of the rasher.
4. Stir the tofu and bacon into the beans.

Selections per serving:
   2 Bread
   2 Fat
   3 Protein
   5 Optional Calories

PARSNIP-TOPPED PIE

SERVES 1

460 CALORIES PER SERVING

This makes a filling meal for a cold day.

1 teaspoon vegetable oil

½ onion, chopped

¼ teaspoon oregano

½ teaspoon chilli sauce

1 small (8oz/227g) can chopped tomatoes

6oz (180g) drained freshly cooked or canned kidney beans

6oz (180g) parsnips

salt

2 tablespoons skimmed milk

1oz (30g) mature Cheddar cheese, grated

> **Tip:**
> The base of this pie can be made in advance and just heated through, topped with the parsnip mixture and grilled when required.

1. Heat the oil in a saucepan, add the onion and stir-fry for 3–4 minutes.
2. Stir the oregano, chilli sauce and tomatoes into the saucepan, bring to the boil and partially cover. Reduce the heat and simmer for 10 minutes.
3. Add the kidney beans, stir round, then partially cover the saucepan and simmer for about 10 minutes until fairly thick.
4. Cut the parsnips into chunks and cook in boiling salted water until tender, about 12–13 minutes, drain.
5. Mash the parsnips until smooth, then stir in the milk.
6. Spoon the beans and tomatoes into a small flameproof dish, then spoon the parsnips over the top and sprinkle with the cheese.
7. Place under a preheated hot grill for 2–3 minutes until golden.

Selections per serving:
  1 Fat
  3 Protein
  5 Vegetable
  15 Optional Calories

TOSTADOS

SERVES 1

285 CALORIES PER SERVING

Tortillas used to be sold only at speciality shops but now the traditional Mexican corn and wheat tortillas are stocked by many super-markets.

1 large tomato

1 tortilla

1 tablespoon tomato purée

1 tablespoon chopped onion

1½oz (45g) cooked ham, diced

1oz (30g) Caerphilly or Cheshire cheese

Tip:
Wheat tortillas are not sold separately so freeze the remainder for future use.

1. Place the tomato in a small bowl, cover with boiling water, leave for 30–40 seconds, drain, slip the skin off and roughly chop.
2. Lay the tortilla flat in a frying pan and heat gently – there is no need to add any oil.
3. Spread the warm tortilla with the tomato purée, arrange the chopped tomato on top, scatter the onion and ham over the tomato and crumble the cheese over evenly.
4. Place the layered tortilla in the frying pan under a hot grill and cook until the topping is hot and the cheese melted. Slide onto a serving plate.

Selections per serving:
1 Bread
2½ Protein
1 Vegetable
10 Optional Calories

PRAWNS WITH RICE

SERVES 1

440 CALORIES PER SERVING

Basmati rice is particularly good for this recipe – it imparts a slightly nutty flavour.

2–3 strands of saffron

1½ teaspoons oil

½ clove garlic, finely chopped

2 tablespoons onion, finely chopped

½ red pepper, seeded and chopped

2oz (60g) long-grain rice

1½ tablespoons chopped dill

salt and pepper

1 egg

2½oz (75g) peeled prawns

Tip:
Store saffron in a dark, airtight container in a cool cupboard – this will help retain its flavour and colour.

1. Put the saffron in a cup or small basin, cover with 3 tablespoons of hot water and leave for 2–3 hours, or longer if possible, to infuse.
2. Heat the oil in a saucepan, add the garlic and onion and stir-fry for 1–2 minutes.
3. Add the red pepper, stir round, then cover the saucepan and leave over a low heat for 4–5 minutes.
4. Stir the rice and dill into the vegetables. Make the saffron water up to the amount given in the rice packaging instructions. Add the saffron and water to the saucepan, season well and cook as described in the instructions.
5. While the rice is cooking place the egg in a saucepan of cold water, bring to the boil and boil for 10 minutes. Place under running cold water, tap and remove the shell – this will prevent a dark line forming round the yolk.
6. When the rice is cooked add the prawns and stir for 1–2 minutes to heat through. Quarter or roughly chop the hot hard-boiled egg and add to the prawns and rice.

Selections per serving:
   2 Bread
   1½ Fat
   3½ Protein
   1 Vegetable

SARDINE SUPPER

SERVES 1

475 CALORIES PER SERVING

Fresh sardines are widely available in fish-mongers and supermarkets – if fresh are not available you can use frozen. Three medium-sized sardines will provide about 3oz (90g) boneless cooked fish.

1 small clove garlic

½ onion

2 tomatoes

6oz (180g) potatoes

2 teaspoons olive oil

5 tablespoons stock

1 teaspoon finely chopped parsley

salt and pepper

3 × 1½oz (45g) sardines, cleaned, gutted and heads removed

Tip:
If fresh herbs are available add a little basil and/or marjoram.

1. Finely chop the garlic and onion. Cover the tomatoes with boiling water, leave 30–40 seconds then remove, slip the skins off and chop the tomatoes. Peel the potatoes, cut into thin slices, then cut each slice into three.
2. Heat the oil in a saucepan, add the garlic and onion and stir-fry over a low to moderate heat for 4–5 minutes.
3. Stir the tomatoes and potatoes into the saucepan and add the stock and parsley. Season well with salt and pepper. Cover the saucepan and leave over a low heat for 10 minutes.
4. Stir the tomatoes and potatoes, lay the sardines on top, cover the saucepan and leave to simmer gently for 10 minutes.
5. Remove the cooked sardines with a fish slice or slotted spoon, increase the heat and boil the tomato mixture for 1 minute, then spoon the vegetables round the sardines.

Selections per serving:
2 Bread
2 Fat
3 Protein
2½ Vegetable
5 Optional Calories

AUTUMN CRISP DESSERT

SERVES 1

150 CALORIES PER SERVING

If the plums are very tart add a little extra sugar or sweetener – but don't forget to add the extra calories (20 per teaspoon) to the total.

1 medium dessert apple

2 medium plums

2–3 tablespoons water

2 teaspoons sugar

½oz (15g) fresh breadcrumbs

Tip:
The sugar and breadcrumb mixture is a suitable topping for a wide variety of fruits.

1. Peel, quarter and core the apple. Cut each quarter in half to make eight pieces of apple.
2. Cut the plums in half, remove the stones and cut into quarters. If the stones are securely attached leave them in place or the plums will not retain their shape.
3. Place the apple and plums in a small saucepan and add just enough water to cover the base of the saucepan. Cover the pan and cook over a very low heat so the fruit is cooked but retains its shape.
4. Using a slotted spoon transfer the cooked fruit to a ramekin and sprinkle with ½–1 teaspoon of sugar.
5. If the saucepan contains more than 1–2 tablespoons of liquid, boil hard to reduce. Spoon the cooking liquid into the ramekin.
6. Mix the breadcrumbs with the remaining sugar, sprinkle over the fruit, place under a preheated grill and cook until golden.

Selections per serving:
½ Bread
2 Fruit
40 Optional Calories

DOUBLE DESSERT

SERVES 1

270 CALORIES PER SERVING

This recipe, a baked apple and baked custard, makes an ideal pudding for Beef Stew (page 173) as all the dishes are cooked at the same temperature.

For the apple:

1 medium cooking apple

½oz (15g) sultanas

¼ teaspoon allspice

¼ teaspoon sugar

2 tablespoons water

For the custard:

¼ teaspoon margarine

¼ pint (150ml) skimmed milk

1 egg

2 teaspoons caster sugar

¼ teaspoon vanilla essence

Tip:
A test to check if the custard is cooked is to insert the tip of a knife into the middle of the custard, then gently press each side of the slit. If the custard is set no liquid will run from the slit.

1. Use an apple corer to remove the core from the apple. Cut about ½ inch (1.25cm) from the bottom of the core and replace in the apple – this will prevent the filling falling out.
2. Mix the sultanas, allspice and sugar together.
3. Score round the centre of the apple and place in an ovenproof dish, press the stuffing in the centre and add the water. Bake at 325°F, 160°C, Gas Mark 3 for about 1 hour.
4. To make the custard: grease a ½ pint (300ml) ovenproof dish with the margarine.
5. Beat a little milk with the egg and sugar – the custard will be fairly sweet in contrast to the apple. Heat the remaining milk until steaming.
6. Pour the hot milk into the beaten egg, add the vanilla essence then strain into the greased dish.
7. Stand the custard in a larger dish containing hot water to a depth of ½ inch (1.25cm,. Bake at 325°F, 160°C, Gas Mark 3 for about 35 minutes until just set.

Selections per serving:
¼ Fat
1½ Fruit
½ Milk
1 Protein
45 Optional Calories

SWEET SOUFFLÉ OMELETTE

SERVES 1

225 CALORIES PER SERVING

This dessert won't keep so make it just before eating.

1 large egg

1 tablespoon skimmed milk

1 teaspoon caster sugar

pinch of cream of tartar

1½ tablespoons jam

1 teaspoon margarine

½ teaspoon icing sugar

Tip:
The sugar may be omitted from the omelette and a savoury filling used in place of the jam to make a snack meal.

1. Separate the egg: place the yolk in a basin with the skimmed milk and caster sugar, and place the egg white in a separate basin with the cream of tartar.
2. Spoon the jam into a small basin and stand in a saucepan of simmering water so it will be warm by the time the omelette is cooked. Alternatively, if you have a microwave oven it can be heated for a few seconds.
3. Beat the egg yolk, milk and caster sugar well together.
4. Whisk the egg white and cream of tartar until peaking, fold the egg yolk mixture through the whisked white.
5. Heat the margarine in a small frying or omelette pan, about 7 inches (17.5cm) in diameter. Spoon the egg mixture into the pan and cook over a moderate heat until the underside is golden – use a palette knife to lift the edge of the omelette gently.
6. Transfer the pan to a hot grill and cook for 1–2 minutes until the mixture has set.
7. Spread the warm jam over half the omelette, fold in half and dust with sieved icing sugar. Slide onto a serving plate and serve immediately.

Selections per serving:
1 Fat
1 Protein
110 Optional Calories

SUNFLOWER SUNDAE

SERVES 1

110 CALORIES PER SERVING

When you feel like giving yourself a treat make this attractive dessert – it only takes a few minutes to assemble.

1oz (30g) curd cheese

1 tablespoon low-fat natural yogurt

½ teaspoon honey

approximately ¼ teaspoon orange flower water

1 medium tangerine, satsuma or clementine

1 kiwi fruit

½ teaspoon coconut

Tip:
To measure ½ teaspoon of honey accurately, lightly grease a ½ teaspoon measure then add the honey. The grease will prevent the honey from sticking to the bowl of the spoon.

1. Mix the curd cheese, yogurt and honey together in a small bowl. Add the orange flower water a few drops at a time as the strength of flavour varies.
2. Peel the tangerine then, very carefully, remove as much of the white membrane as possible from the outside of each segment. Gently pull the segments apart from the top so they are held together at the base and fan out into a water-lily shape.
3. Place the open tangerine on a small serving plate. Peel and thinly slice the kiwi fruit, then arrange overlapping slices round the tangerine.
4. Spoon the curd cheese mixture into the centre of the tangerine. Toast the coconut under a moderate grill until golden then sprinkle over the curd cheese.

Selections per serving:
1½ Fruit
½ Protein
25 Optional Calories

GUESTS ARE COMING

Successful entertaining, no matter what the occasion, depends on organisation and preparation. This section is primarily included as a guide for organising a dinner party but a few recipes are included for quick snacks or afternoon tea.

Before planning a meal invite the guests and give them time to reply so you will know how many people to cook for and if they have any preferences or dislikes regarding food. Only then can you think about the menu, quantities and so on.

Choose recipes and courses which complement each other: a good dinner party should leave the guests feeling relaxed and well, not over-fed.

If you want to serve a rich dessert plan a light starter such as Melon with Figs (page 198) or just a slice of melon. Work out quantities carefully and remember some recipes can't just be altered to suit the number you require. A recipe such as Baked Cheesecake (page 212) will serve up to twelve people but if more servings are required the whole recipe must be doubled. Consider which recipes and accompaniments can be prepared in advance so you are able to spend time with your guests. It may be sensible to serve an attractive mixed salad or a selection of salads with the main course; this will save cooking vegetables while eating the starter. Always include at least one cold course which can be prepared well ahead of time and successfully stored in the refrigerator or freezer. Don't be over-ambitious; cook dishes which are within your own scope. Check ingredients are easily available, for example lamb fillets are delicious in the spring when lamb is really tender but would be tough during the winter months.

Before making shopping lists of ingredients consider how the food should be garnished and the table made attractive. Herbs, fruit, leaves and flowers can transform everyday dishes into spectacular centrepieces. An attractive table helps to create a special atmosphere. Use a tablecloth which hangs about 10 inches (25cm) from the table, very clean cutlery, china and glass, pretty napkins and, if you wish, a centrepiece such as a small flower decoration or candles. Only when you have planned all of this will you be able to make detailed shopping lists, place orders for particular foods and arrange to borrow or hire china, glass, etc.

Don't rely on your memory for cleaning the room, laying the table, collecting orders and preparing food. Write a detailed checklist and cross off each job as it is completed. Leave plenty of time to change and get yourself ready, put on music and so on, and when your guests arrive make sure you have time to spend with them. By carefully following your timeplan you will know when to remove food from the refrigerator, put heat under saucepans, turn the oven on – and enjoy the party.

GUESTS ARE COMING

All recipes marked * are suitable for vegetarians as well as non-vegetarians

MINESTRONE

SERVES 6

160 CALORIES PER SERVING

A really thick hearty soup suitable for a winter's lunch.

2 teaspoons olive oil

1 large onion, roughly chopped

2 carrots, diced

2 sticks celery, diced

2 teaspoons chopped basil

1 small (8oz/227g) can chopped tomatoes

3oz (90g) dwarf green beans, cut in 1-inch (2.5-cm) lengths

9oz (270g) drained canned chick peas, liquid reserved

2 pints (1.2 litre) stock

3oz (90g) thin macaroni or small pasta shapes

2 tablespoons chopped parsley

1½oz (45g) Parmesan cheese, finely grated

1. Heat the oil in a large saucepan, add the onion and stir-fry for 3 minutes.
2. Stir the carrots, celery, basil, tomatoes, beans, chick peas and their liquid and stock into the saucepan and bring to the boil. Reduce the heat, cover the saucepan and leave to simmer for about 40 minutes.
3. Stir the macaroni into the saucepan and boil for about 8 minutes or until cooked.
4. To serve: ladle the soup into warm soup bowls and sprinkle with the chopped parsley and grated cheese.

Selections per serving:
½ Bread
¾ Protein
1½ Vegetable
15 Optional Calories

Tip:
Store a small piece of Parmesan cheese in the refrigerator. It keeps well and has a much better flavour than the dried Parmesan sold in cartons.

VICHYSSOISE

SERVES 8

115 CALORIES PER SERVING

This soup can be made in advance and stored in the refrigerator.

2 tablespoons margarine

12oz (360g) leeks, sliced

1 onion, roughly chopped

9oz (270g) potatoes, roughly chopped

1¼ pints (750ml) well flavoured vegetable or chicken stock

8fl oz (240ml) skimmed milk

salt and pepper

8 tablespoons single cream

2 tablespoons chopped chives

Tip:
Although this is traditionally served chilled it can be reheated, ladled into warm soup bowls and then the cream swirled on top and sprinkled with chives.

1. Melt the margarine in a medium-sized saucepan, add the leeks, onion and potatoes and stir round for 1–2 minutes. Cover the saucepan and leave over a low heat for about 15 minutes or until the leeks and onion are limp.
2. Stir the stock and milk into the vegetables and season with salt and pepper. Cover the saucepan and leave over a low heat for 30 minutes.
3. Allow the soup to cool then transfer to a food processor or liquidiser and process to a smooth purée.
4. Chill the soup until ready to serve. Adjust the seasoning, adding more salt and pepper as necessary. Ladle the soup into eight soup bowls and swirl a tablespoon of single cream in each. Sprinkle with the chopped chives.

Selections per serving:
¼ Bread
¾ Fat
¾ Vegetable
55 Optional Calories

MELON WITH FIGS

SERVES 4

30 CALORIES PER SERVING

This attractive and appetising hors d'œuvre *can be prepared in advance, covered and refrigerated.*

½ medium charentais melon

2 large figs

¼-inch (5-mm) root ginger

juice of ½ a medium orange

2 teaspoons finely chopped mint

4 sprigs of mint

Tip:
To obtain the full flavour of the fruit, remove from the refrigerator 30–40 minutes before serving.

1. Cut the melon in half and scoop out all its seeds. Remove the skin from each piece of melon then cut across its width into thin slices.
2. Cut the figs into the same number of slices as the melon – there is no need to remove the figs' skins.
3. Cut away and discard the outer skin of the ginger then place in a garlic press and extract as much juice as possible. Mix the ginger juice, orange juice and chopped mint together.
4. Arrange alternate slices of melon and fig on four serving plates, spoon over the minty ginger dressing then garnish each serving with a sprig of mint.

Selections per serving:
¾ Fruit
10 Optional Calories

TROUT LOGS

SERVES 4

180 CALORIES PER SERVING

Serve this starter with sharp knives so the trout is easily cut without squashing the filling.

3oz (90g) thin slices of smoked trout

1 hard-boiled egg

2oz (60g) cottage cheese

½ teaspoon chopped chives

2½ tablespoons double cream

2 teaspoons horseradish sauce

few chicory, endive or lettuce leaves

4 × 1oz (30g) slices wholemeal bread

4 teaspoons low-fat spread

Tip:
Some prepacked frozen cream is separated into 1 tablespoon pieces; these are well worth keeping in the freezer.

1. Cut the trout into four strips – if necessary overlap two pieces so all four strips are more or less the same size.
2. Roughly chop the egg then sieve the egg and cottage cheese.
3. Stir the chives into the sieved mixture.
4. Spoon the egg and cheese onto each strip of trout and spread evenly along the lengths.
5. Loosely roll up the trout. Transfer the trout to four serving plates.
6. Using a fork whisk the cream until thick and stir in the horseradish sauce. Spoon the horseradish cream on each Trout Log and roughen the surface with a fork. Decorate each plate with the salad leaves.
7. Spread the bread with low-fat spread, cut each slice into four triangles and serve with the logs.

Selections per serving:
1 Bread
½ Fat
1¼ Protein
40 Optional Calories

BEEF WITH PRUNES

SERVES 6

240 CALORIES PER SERVING

If pickling onions aren't available substitute one large, roughly chopped onion.

12 small stoned prunes

4fl oz (120ml) red wine

1lb 12oz (840g) braising steak

¼ teaspoon ground allspice

12fl oz (360ml) beef stock

6oz (180g) small pickling onions, halved

6oz (180g) small button mushrooms

Tip:
Bake six jacket potatoes in the same oven to accompany this dish.

---

1. Soak the prunes overnight, or for several hours, in the red wine.
2. Lay the beef on the rack of a grill pan and grill under a moderate heat, turning once, until the fat stops dripping. Cut the beef into six pieces.
3. Place the beef, prunes and wine, allspice, stock and vegetables in an ovenproof dish, stir all the ingredients together, cover and cook in a moderate oven 350°F, 180°C, Gas Mark 4 for 1½–2 hours until the beef is tender. Stir two or three times during the cooking time.

Selections per serving:
½ Fruit
3½ Protein
¾ Vegetable
15 Optional Calories

MOULES MARINIÈRES

SERVES 4

120 CALORIES PER SERVING

The careful preparation of mussels prior to cooking is essential. They must be alive and remain shut when in cold water or tapped. Mussels which remain shut when cooked must be discarded.

2 pints (I litre) or I½–I¾lbs (720–840g) live mussels

I shallot, very finely chopped

4fl oz (120ml) white wine

4fl oz (120ml) water

2 tablespoons finely chopped parsley

4 teaspoons margarine

2 tablespoons flour

salt and pepper

chopped parsley

Tip:
If the mussels have to be kept overnight, place them in a bowl of cold water and add a handful of oatmeal.

1. Wash and scrub the mussels well under running cold water. As the mussels are prepared place them in a bowl of cold water.
2. Pull off the molluscs or any weed hanging from the mussel shells and place in a second bowl of cold water. Transfer all the mussels to the second bowl by hand – this prevents any sand tipping from one bowl to another. If the mussels feel heavy discard or prise them open and remove any sand they may contain. If a mussel remains open discard it.
3. Place the shallot, wine, water, prepared mussels and I tablespoon parsley in a large saucepan. Cover and place over a moderate heat. Simmer for 2 minutes, shaking the pan from time to time – the mussels should open wide. Do not overcook or the mussels will be tough.
4. Using a slotted spoon remove the mussels from the liquid and boil the liquor for 2 minutes.
5. In a separate saucepan melt the margarine, stir in the flour and remove from the heat.
6. Discard any mussels which haven't opened during cooking. Remove the top shells from all the remaining mussels and arrange them on four warm serving plates.
7. Gradually blend the cooking liquor into the margarine and flour with the remaining parsley. Bring to the boil, stirring all the time. Boil for I minute, season, then pour over the mussels, sprinkle with parsley and serve.

Selections per serving:
  I Fat
  I ½ Protein
  40 Optional Calories

CHICKEN STROGANOFF

SERVES 4

320 CALORIES PER SERVING

This tastes delicious but lacks colour so serve it with brightly coloured vegetables such as carrots and mange-tout.

I large onion

8oz (240g) button mushrooms

IIb 4oz (600g) boneless skinned chicken breasts

2 tablespoons margarine

salt and pepper

10 tablespoons soured cream

I tablespoon chopped parsley

Tip:
Serve a light white wine with this dish.

1. Roughly chop the onion. Halve or thickly slice the mushrooms and cut the chicken into ½-inch (1.25-cm) strips.
2. Heat 2 teaspoons margarine in a saucepan, add the onion and stir-fry for 2 minutes. Cover the saucepan, reduce the heat and leave the onion to steam for 5 minutes. Using a slotted spoon transfer the onion to a plate.
3. Add the remaining margarine to the saucepan and melt over a low heat. Add the chicken strips and stir-fry for 6–8 minutes until it loses its pinkness.
4. Return the onion to the saucepan, add the mushrooms and stir well. Cover the saucepan and leave for 4–5 minutes.
5. Transfer the chicken, onion and mushrooms to a plate and keep warm. Increase the heat as high as possible and boil the liquid rapidly until reduced to about 3 tablespoons. Stir in the chicken mixture with the reduced liquid, season well with salt and pepper, stir in the soured cream, sprinkle with parsley and serve.

Selections per serving:
I ½ Fat
4 Protein
I ¼ Vegetable
85 Optional Calories

CHRISTMAS DINNER

SERVES 10

The following recipes give individual calorie counts for the Stuffed Turkey with Gravy, Bread Sauce and Cranberry and Port Sauce. This enables you to choose whether to have the turkey with bread, cranberry sauce, or both.

BREAD SAUCE

SERVES 10

50 CALORIES PER PERSON

I onion

4 whole cloves

few peppercorns

blade of mace (optional)

¾ pint (450ml) whole milk

3oz (90g) fresh breadcrumbs

salt

Tip:
This sauce can be prepared as far as the end of 'Point I' until you are ready to serve.

1. Peel the onion and press the cloves into it. Place the onion, peppercorns and mace in a small saucepan. Pour in the milk and heat very gently until the milk is steaming and just reaching boiling point. Remove from the heat and leave for 30 minutes.
2. Remove the peppercorns, mace and onion. Stir in the breadcrumbs and return to a very low heat. Bring to the boil, stirring all the time. Remove the onion, season with salt, and serve.

Selections per serving:
    ¼ Bread
    ¼ Milk
    25 Optional Calories

STUFFED TURKEY
WITH GRAVY

280 CALORIES PER SERVING — BASED ON 3½OZ (105G) OF TURKEY PER SERVING AND ALL THE STUFFING BEING USED

11½–12½lbs (5.5–6kg) fresh turkey with giblets

1 large onion, plus a few extra slices

2½ tablespoons margarine

1 tablespoon cornflour

Stuffing:

2oz (60g) dried apricots

8 large prunes

9oz (270g) dry bread

2 large onions

8oz (240g) cooking apple

2½ tablespoons margarine

1 large egg, beaten

Tip:
Always leave roast turkey or chicken to stand for about 10 minutes. This makes carving much easier.

Selections per serving:
    ¾ Bread
    1½ Fat
    ¾ Fruit
    3½ Protein
    ¼ Vegetable
    25 Optional Calories

1. Prepare the stuffing: place the dried apricots and prunes in a bowl, cover with boiling water and leave for 3–4 hours or overnight. Drain, remove the stones from the prunes and roughly chop the fruit.
2. Break the bread into pieces, place in a liquidiser or food processor and process to make breadcrumbs.
3. Chop the onions and peel, core and grate the apple.
4. Heat the margarine in a large saucepan, add the onion and stir-fry for 5–6 minutes. Remove from the heat and stir in all the remaining stuffing ingredients.
5. Remove the giblets from the turkey, rinse under cold running water and pat dry with kitchen paper. Put the giblets in an ovenproof dish with a few slices of onion, and add about 1 pint (600ml) water to cover. Cover and transfer to the lowest shelf in the oven.
6. Spoon the stuffing into the skin at the neck end of the turkey. Place the onion in the body of the bird. Skew through the turkey to hold the wings in place. Secure the drumsticks. Alternatively use fine string to truss the bird. Transfer to a rack standing in a large roasting tin.
7. Spread the margarine all over the turkey and thickly over the breast. Cover with foil and cook at 400–425°F, 200–210°C, Gas Mark 6–7 for 3 hours 15 minutes. Remove the foil, baste with the juices and continue cooking, uncovered, for 30–40 minutes until brown. Transfer to a warm plate and leave to stand while preparing the gravy.
8. Blend the cornflour to a smooth paste with a little cold water. Place the giblets and juices from the roasting pan into a basin and stand it in a bowl of chilled water – if possible add a few ice cubes to the chilled water. As soon as the fat solidifies on the top, skim it off. Strain the giblets and gradually stir the juices into the cornflour. Pour into a saucepan and bring to the boil, stirring all the time. Boil for 2 minutes, pour into a gravy boat or jug.
9. Carve the turkey, allowing 3½oz (105g) per person. Serve the turkey with stuffing and gravy but remember to remove the turkey skin which will contain a high proportion of fat.

Christmas Dinner

CRANBERRY AND PORT SAUCE

SERVES 10

20 CALORIES PER SERVING

8oz (240g) cranberries

¼ pint (150ml) water

1 teaspoon arrowroot or cornflour

2 tablespoons sugar

3 tablespoons port

Tip:
Make this sauce on Christmas Eve.

1. Place the cranberries and water in a small saucepan over a moderate heat. Simmer for 10–15 minutes until the cranberries are cooked. Stir briskly to break up some of the cranberries to make a purée containing a few whole cranberries.
2. Blend the arrowroot or cornflour to a smooth paste with 2–3 teaspoons cold water. Stir into the cranberries and bring to the boil, stirring all the time. Boil for 2 minutes.
3. Remove the sauce from the heat and stir in the sugar and port. Serve hot or leave until cool.

Selections per serving:
20 Optional Calories

 VEGETARIAN

VEGETABLE STIR-FRY

SERVES 4

250 CALORIES PER SERVING

This colourful stir-fry is a very simple recipe suitable for serving to guests.

3oz (90g) fennel

6 spring onions

I red pepper, seeded

I small courgette

6oz (180g) tofu

2 tablespoons tomato purée

3 tablespoons sherry

2 tablespoons soy sauce

2 tablespoons oil

I clove garlic, finely chopped

2 teaspoons finely chopped ginger

3oz (90g) mange-tout

6oz (180g) drained canned sweetcorn

8oz (240g) beansprouts

2oz (60g) dry roasted peanuts

Tip:
To make a complete meal, serve with plain or saffron rice.

1. Thinly slice the fennel and spring onions.
2. Cut the red pepper, courgette and tofu into ½-inch (1.25-cm) strips.
3. Blend the tomato purée together with the sherry and soy sauce.
4. Heat the oil in a wok or saucepan. Add the garlic and ginger and stir-fry for 1–2 minutes.
5. Add the spring onions, red pepper and fennel and stir-fry for 4–5 minutes.
6. Stir the courgette, mange-tout, tofu and sweetcorn into the stir-fried vegetables. Continue stirring over a high heat for 2 minutes; don't worry if the tofu breaks up.
7. Add the blended tomato purée, beansprouts and peanuts, stir-fry for 1–2 minutes.

Selections per serving:
½ Bread
2 Fat
1½ Protein
2 Vegetable
15 Optional Calories

SALMON RING

SERVES 4

155 CALORIES PER SERVING

To enable you to spend time with your guests, this recipe may be made in advance.

7½oz (212g) can red salmon

8oz (240g) cottage cheese

¼ pint (150ml) skimmed milk

2 teaspoons chopped chives

grated zest of ¼ of a lemon

I sachet gelatine

slices of lemon and cucumber

Tip:
If you have a 1 pint (600ml) ring mould an attractive salad can be arranged in the centre of the ring.

1. Drain and reserve the juices from the can of salmon. Place the salmon, cottage cheese and milk in a blender and process until smooth.
2. Pour the salmon and cheese mixture into a bowl and stir in the chives and lemon zest.
3. Place the reserved salmon juices in a cup, sprinkle in the gelatine and stir. Stand the cup in a saucepan of simmering water and leave until the gelatine has dissolved.
4. Stir the dissolved gelatine into the salmon and cheese mixture and spoon into a 1 pint (600ml) wetted mould. Chill until set.
5. To serve: dip the mould in hot water and invert onto a serving plate, then garnish with the slices of lemon and cucumber.

Selections per serving:
2½ Protein
10 Optional Calories

CHEESE SOUFFLÉ

SERVES 4

225 CALORIES PER SERVING

This is suitable to serve as a starter for four people or as a snack lunch for two.

4 teaspoons margarine

½oz (15g) flour

¼ pint (150ml) skimmed milk

3 eggs, separated

1½oz (45g) Cheddar cheese, grated

1½oz (45g) Parmesan cheese, grated

1 tablespoon chopped chives or spring onions

salt and pepper

good pinch of powdered mustard

Tip:
Always serve soufflés immediately – the minute they are removed from the oven they begin to sink.

1. Use a little of the margaine to grease a 6-inch (15-cm) soufflé dish.
2. Heat the remaining margarine in a 2-pint (1-litre 200-ml) saucepan, add the flour and cook over a low heat for 1–2 minutes, stirring all the time.
3. Remove from the heat and gradually blend in the milk. Bring to the boil, stirring continuously, and boil for 1 minute.
4. Allow to cool for 1–2 minutes then beat in the egg yolks, cheeses and chives. Season to taste with salt, pepper and mustard.
5. Whisk the egg whites with a pinch of salt until peaking. Lightly fold them into the cheese sauce using a tablespoon. Transfer the mixture to the soufflé dish and bake at 350°F, 180°C, Gas Mark 4 for about 35 minutes until golden brown, well risen and just set. Serve immediately.

Selections per serving:
   1 Fat
   1½ Protein
   25 Optional Calories

BAKED CHEESECAKE

SERVES 12

190 CALORIES PER SERVING

This cheesecake has a completely different flavour and appearance from the uncooked variety. It must be left until completely cold before removing from the tin. Its texture is crumbly but mousse-like.

3oz (90g) plain flour

pinch salt

2 tablespoons margarine

approximately 1 tablespoon ice-cold water

1lb (480g) curd cheese

zest and juice of 1 lemon

10fl oz (300ml) low-fat natural yogurt

3oz (90g) sultanas

½ teaspoon vanilla essence

4 eggs, separated

5 tablespoons caster sugar

1oz (30g) cornflour

pinch of cream of tartar

½ teaspoon icing sugar

Tip:
Don't freeze this cheesecake as the texture will be affected and become very crumbly.

1. Reserve 2 teaspoons of flour. Sieve the remainder with the salt into a bowl. Add the margarine (if possible margarine that has been stored in a freezer) and rub in until the mixture resembles fresh breadcrumbs.

2. Mix the cold water into the pastry with a round-bladed knife then, if time allows, wrap in clingfilm or foil and refrigerate for 10–15 minutes.

3. Line the sides of a deep 8-inch (20-cm) round loose-bottomed cake tin with non-stick baking parchment.

4. Dust the working surface and rolling pin with the reserved flour and roll the pastry out to an 8-inch (20-cm) circle. Line the base of the tin with the pastry. Prick with a fork and bake in a preheated oven at 400°F, 200°C, Gas Mark 6 for 10–12 minutes.

5. Mix the curd cheese, lemon zest and juice, half the yogurt and sultanas together. In a separate bowl mix the vanilla essence and egg yolks. Add the caster sugar, cornflour and a little yogurt and mix to form a smooth paste, then gradually add the remaining yogurt.

6. Gradually beat the egg yolk mixture into the curd cheese.

7. Whisk the egg whites and cream of tartar until peaking, fold into the cheese and spoon onto the pastry in the cake tin. Return to the oven and bake at 300°F, 150°C, Gas Mark 3 for 1½–1¾ hours until firm to touch and turning golden brown.

8. Leave in the tin until completely cold. The cheesecake will gradually sink – don't worry, this is meant to happen! Remove from the tin, slide onto a flat plate and remove the baking parchment. Sieve the icing sugar over the top and serve.

Selections per serving:
¼ Bread
½ Fat
¼ Fruit
1 Protein
50 Optional Calories

BLACK FOREST FEAST

SERVES 4

150 CALORIES PER SERVING

A delicious dessert for a special occasion.

4oz (120g) black cherries, halved and pitted

2 teaspoons brandy or kirsch

2½oz (75g) plain chocolate

2 eggs, separated

pinch of cream of tartar

Tip:
If you prefer, substitute the plain chocolate with milk chocolate, but don't use the white variety.

1. Place the cherries in a small bowl, sprinkle over the brandy or kirsch and leave for 1–2 hours.
2. Break the chocolate into small pieces and place in a bowl. Stand the bowl over a saucepan of simmering water and leave until just melted.
3. Stir the egg yolks into the melted chocolate and stir continuously for 2 minutes. Remove from the heat and leave to cool a little.
4. Spoon the cherries and alcohol into four glasses.
5. Whisk the egg whites and cream of tartar until peaking. Fold a little of the egg white into the melted chocolate then, using a metal spoon, fold in the remaining egg white until evenly mixed. Take care not to stir the mixture or the air will be knocked out and its foamy consistency will be affected.
6. Spoon the chocolate mousse mixture evenly on top of the cherries. Chill until ready to serve.

Selections per serving:
¼ Fruit
½ Protein
100 Optional Calories

STRAWBERRY YOGURT ICE

SERVES 8

50 CALORIES PER SERVING

Make this when strawberries are in season so they will be sweet, juicy and cheap.

10oz (300g) strawberries

3½ tablespoons caster sugar

5fl oz (150ml) low-fat natural yogurt

2 egg whites

pinch of cream of tartar

Tip:
This can be stored for up to 6 weeks in the freezer.

1. Place the strawberries, sugar and yogurt in a food processor or liquidiser and process to form a smooth purée.
2. Pour the purée into a container and freeze for about 3 hours, beating well every 45 minutes to 1 hour to break up the ice crystals.
3. When the purée becomes a smooth thick consistency, place the egg whites and cream of tartar in a bowl and whisk until peaking.
4. Fold about one third of the egg whites into the purée to lighten it, then fold in the remaining whisked egg whites until evenly mixed.
5. Return to the freezer and freeze for several hours or overnight. Place in the refrigerator 30–40 minutes before spooning or scooping into serving dishes.

Selections per serving:
¼ Fruit
40 Optional Calories

Strawberry Yogurt Ice

WHITE CHOCOLATE MOUSSE

SERVES 4

165 CALORIES PER SERVING

This is a very rich dessert so the portions are small. It looks pretty served in small stemmed glasses.

3oz (90g) white chocolate

1 teaspoon skimmed milk

¼ teaspoon peppermint essence

2 large eggs, separated

pinch of cream of tartar

¼oz (10g) plain chocolate, curls or grated

4 tiny sprigs of mint

Tip:
Store eggs with blunt end uppermost so the yolk is kept surrounded by the white.

1. Break the white chocolate and place in a bowl resting on a bowl of simmering water.
2. When the chocolate has melted stir in the milk and peppermint essence, then add the egg yolks and continue stirring for 1–2 minutes.
3. Remove the bowl from the saucepan and leave until the mixture cools a little and begins to thicken.
4. Whisk the egg whites with a pinch of cream of tartar until peaking. Using a metal spoon fold about a quarter of the egg whites into the white chocolate to lighten the mixture. Then carefully fold in the remaining egg white and spoon into four small glasses. Chill until just set.
5. Before serving decorate each glass with the plain chocolate and a sprig of mint.

Selections per serving:
  ½ Protein
  120 Optional Calories

CHOCOLATE SWIRL CAKE

SERVES 12

200 CALORIES PER SERVING

This cake has a marbled chocolate and lemon appearance. If you wish to increase the colours add a little gravy browning or brown colouring to the chocolate mixture and a few drops of yellow colouring to the lemon.

8 tablespoons margarine

7 tablespoons caster sugar

1 tablespoon golden syrup

2 eggs, beaten

8oz (240g) self-raising flour

grated zest of ½ a lemon

1–2 teaspoons lemon juice

1 tablespoon cocoa

Tip:
Make sure the non-stick baking parchment completely covers the base of the tin to prevent sticking.

1. Line a 7-inch (17.5-cm) round cake tin with non-stick baking parchment.
2. Beat the margarine, sugar and syrup together until light and creamy. Gradually add the eggs a little at a time, beating well after each addition. If necessary add a little flour to prevent the mixture curdling.
3. Divide the creamed mixture in half and spoon one half into a separate bowl. Mix the lemon zest and juice into one mixture.
4. Weigh the flour and sieve 4oz (120g) into the lemon mixture and sieve the remainder with the cocoa into the other bowl.
5. Fold the flour into the lemon mixture then, with a clean spoon, fold the cocoa mixture and 2–3 teaspoons of water into the other bowl.
6. Place small spoonfuls of both mixtures over the base of the tin and top with any remaining mixture, then spread evenly, swirling the two colours gently together.
7. Bake at 325°F, 160°C, Gas Mark 3 for about 1 hour 15 minutes until the cake is level and firm to the touch. Leave to cool in the tin for 10 minutes then turn out onto a cooling rack.

Selections per serving:
½ Bread
2 Fat
65 Optional Calories

NUTTY COOKIES

MAKES 12

85 CALORIES PER COOKIE

I find these biscuits really moreish so I only make them when I have guests and can't eat them all!

3 tablespoons crunchy peanut butter

1 tablespoon margarine

4 tablespoons golden syrup

¼ teaspoon vanilla essence

4oz (120g) self-raising flour

½ teaspoon bicarbonate of soda

Tip:
Store these biscuits in an airtight container.

1. Line two baking sheets with non-stick baking parchment.
2. Place the peanut butter, margarine, golden syrup and vanilla essence in a saucepan. Sieve the flour and bicarbonate of soda into a bowl.
3. Gently heat the peanut butter mixture until the peanut butter and margarine have melted.
4. Pour the warm mixture into the flour and bicarbonate of soda and mix well.
5. Roll the mixture into twelve balls, arrange on the baking sheets and slightly flatten each cookie.
6. Bake at 350°F, 180°C, Gas Mark 4 for 15–20 minutes until light brown. Leave on the baking sheet for 3 or 4 minutes then transfer to a cooling rack.

Selections per serving:
¼ Bread
½ Fat
¼ Protein
25 Optional Calories

Nutty Cookies and Twirls

TWIRLS

SERVES 12

85 CALORIES PER BISCUIT

These simple biscuits are quick to make and incorporate ingredients which are usually in the kitchen.

4 tablespoons margarine

2½ tablespoons icing sugar, sieved

finely grated zest of 1 lemon

1oz (30g) cornflour, sieved

2 tablespoons low-fat natural yogurt

1 tablespoon lemon juice

3oz (90g) self-raising flour

Tip:
Store these biscuits on their own – they could cause others to soften.

1. Line a large baking sheet with non-stick baking parchment.
2. Cream the margarine, icing sugar and lemon zest together.
3. Beat the cornflour into the creamed mixture then add the yogurt, lemon juice and self-raising flour and mix well.
4. Spoon the mixture into a piping bag fitted with a ½-inch (1.25-cm) fluted nozzle. Pipe the mixture into twelve 'S' shapes.
5. Bake the Twirls at 375°F, 190°C, Gas Mark 5 for 25 minutes until golden. Transfer to a wire rack and leave to cool.

Selections per serving:
¼ Bread
1 Fat
20 Optional Calories

MARINATED FRUITS

SERVES 4

85 CALORIES PER SERVING

This refreshing dessert doesn't need cream or yogurt, its appearance and flavour is delicious on its own.

2 medium oranges

2 kiwi fruit

4oz (120g) pineapple

5oz (150g) strawberries

½ teaspoon caster sugar

4 tablespoons kirsch

Tip:
If fresh pineapple is unavailable or very expensive, substitute it with the canned variety.

1. Peel the oranges, remove all the pith, cut into thin slices, then cut into halves or quarters. Place in a small bowl.
2. Peel and slice the kiwi fruit and place in a small bowl.
3. Dice the pineapple and place in a small bowl.
4. Slice the strawberries and place in a small bowl, then sprinkle with the sugar.
5. Pour 1 tablespoon of kirsch over each bowl of fruit and leave to stand for at least 4 hours, stirring gently two or three times.
6. Arrange alternate layers of the fruit in four serving glasses and pour over any juices. Chill until ready to serve.

Selections per serving:
1½ Fruit
35 Optional Calories

INDEX